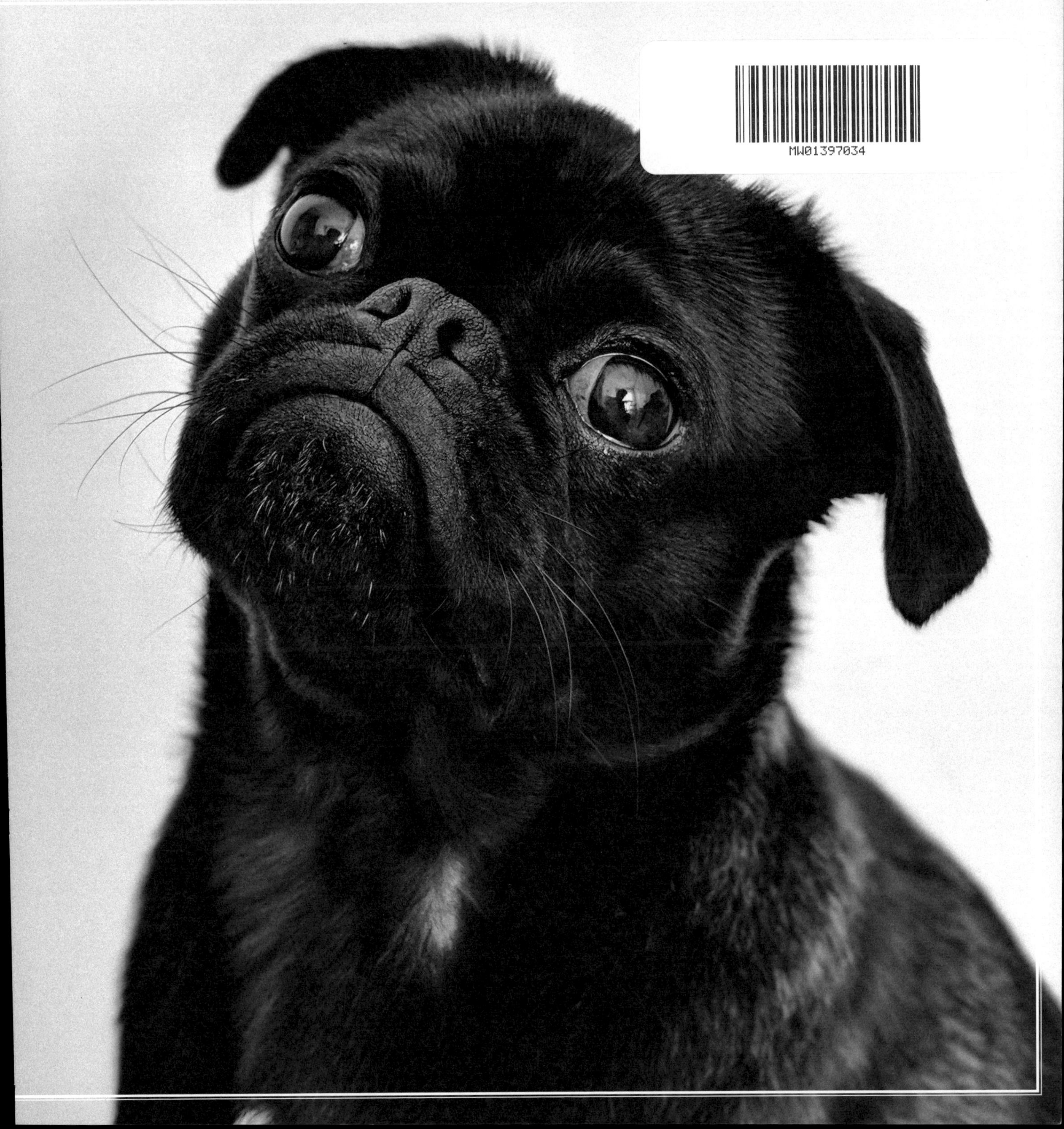

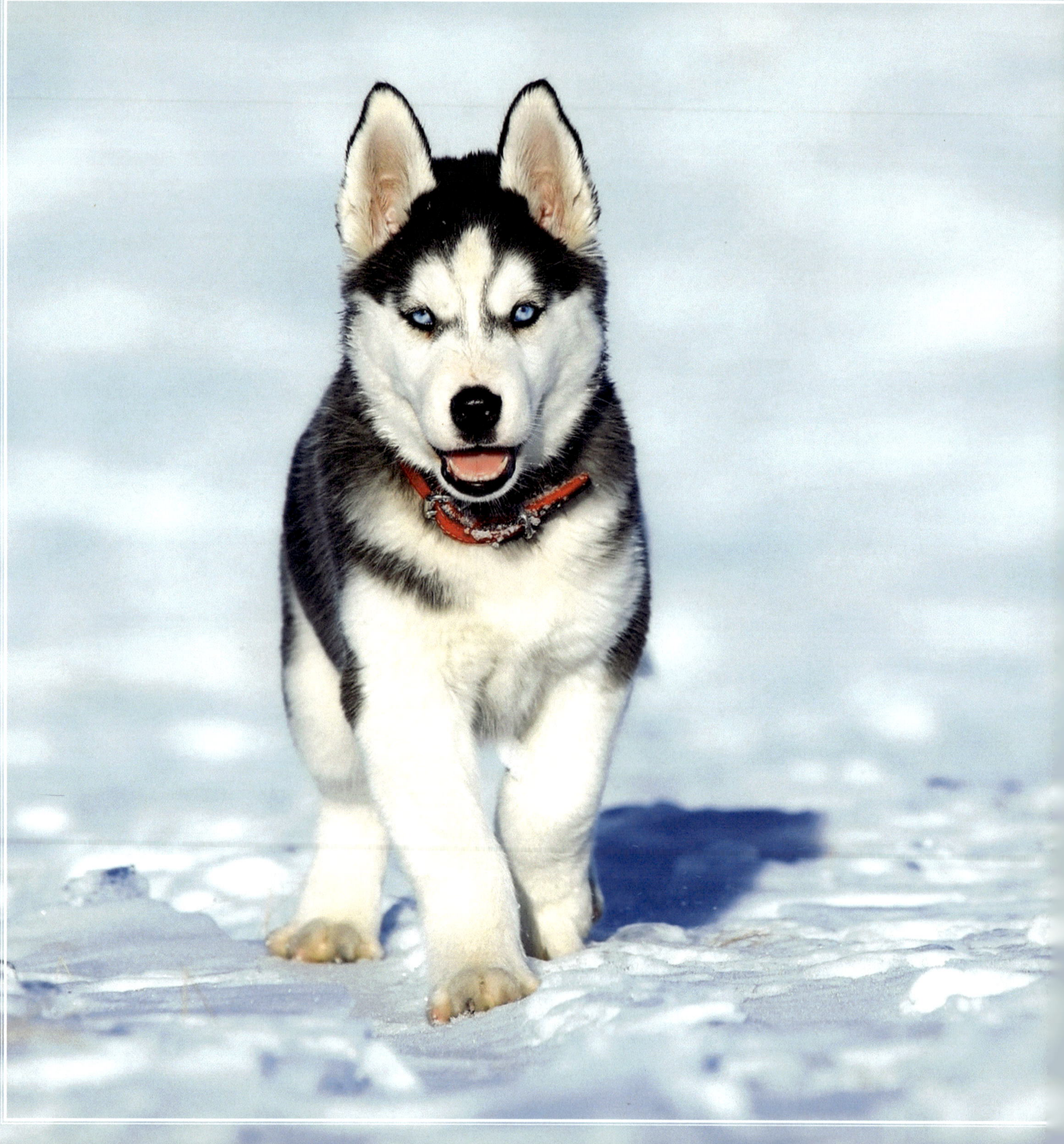

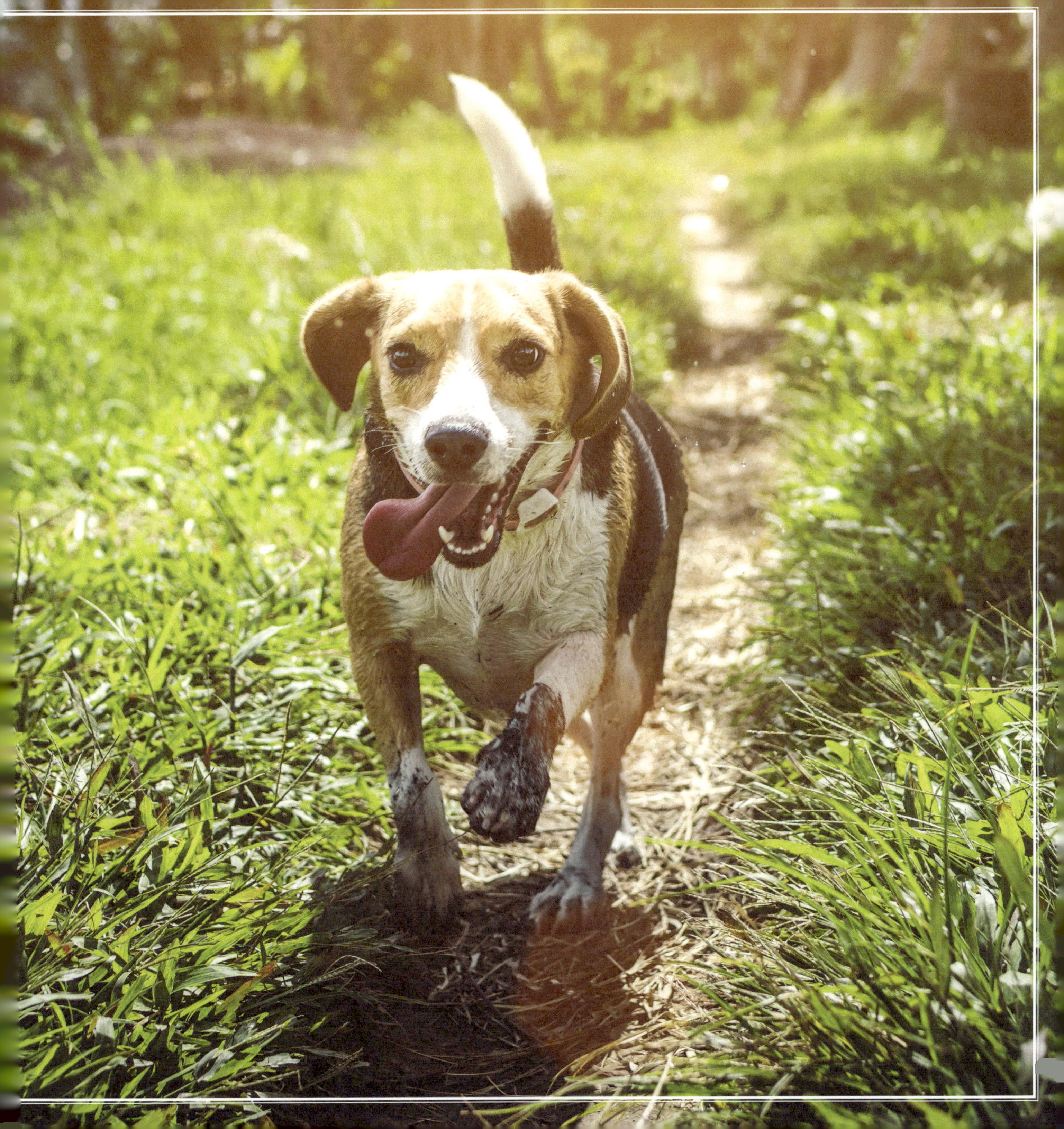

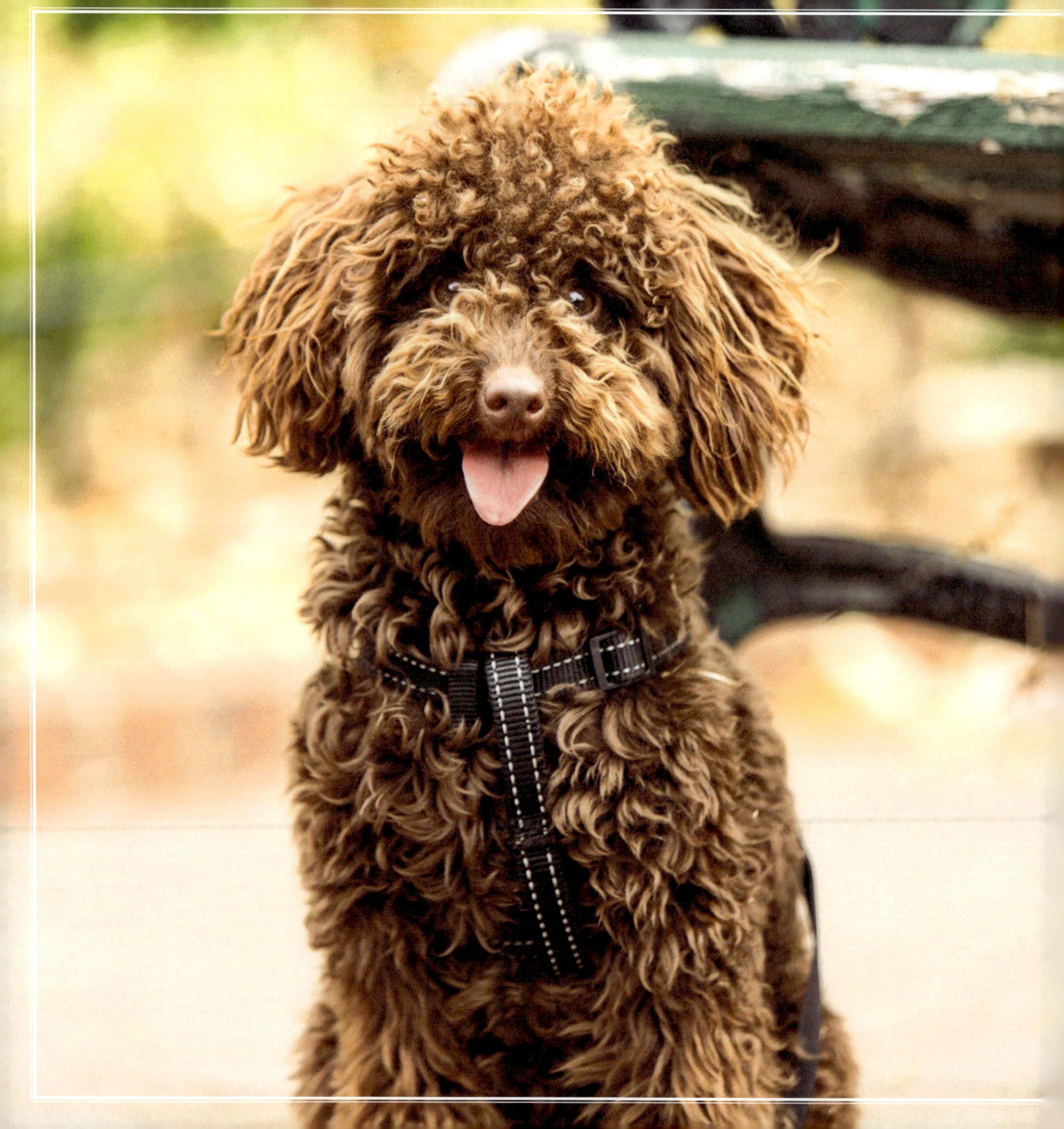

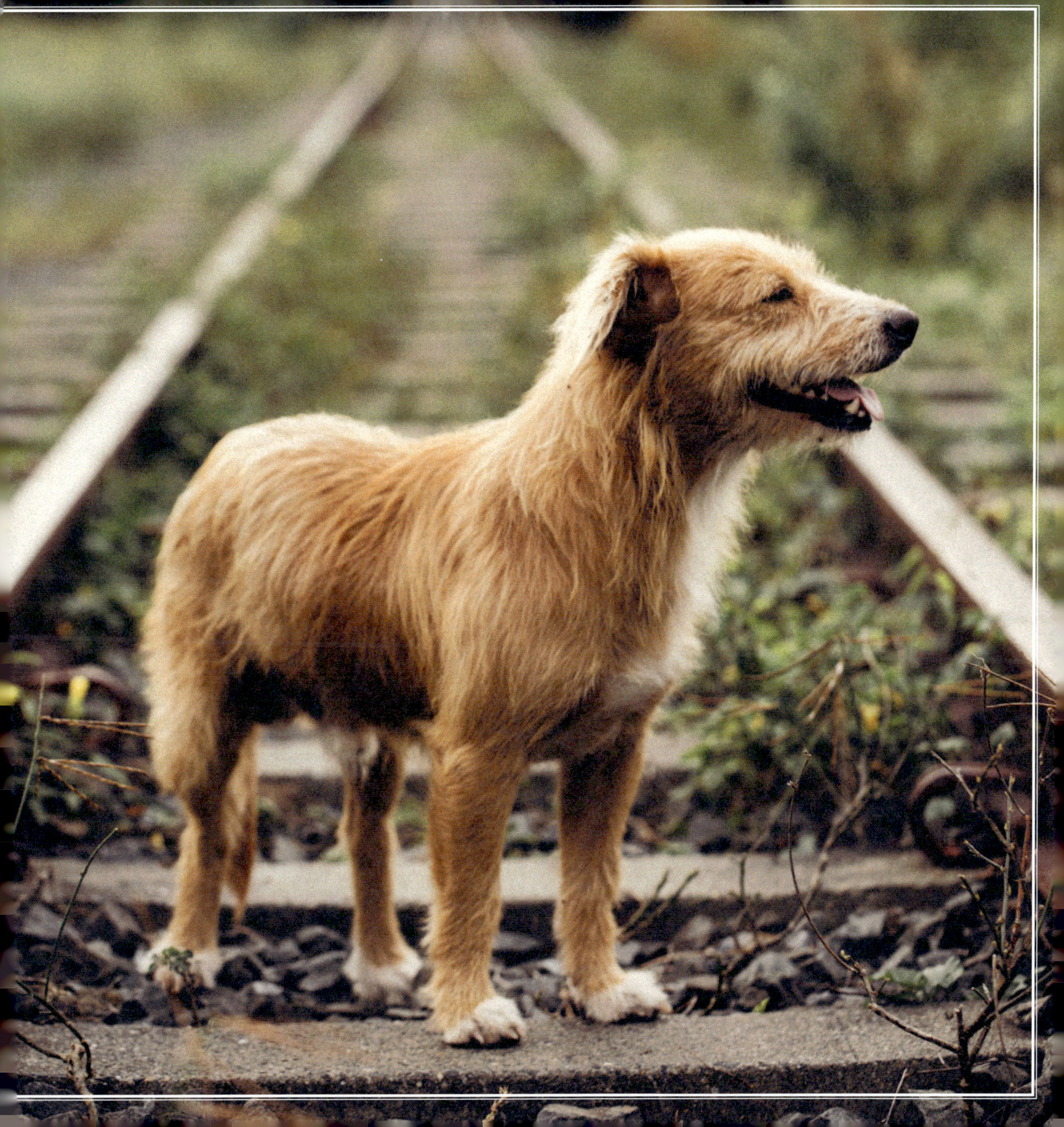

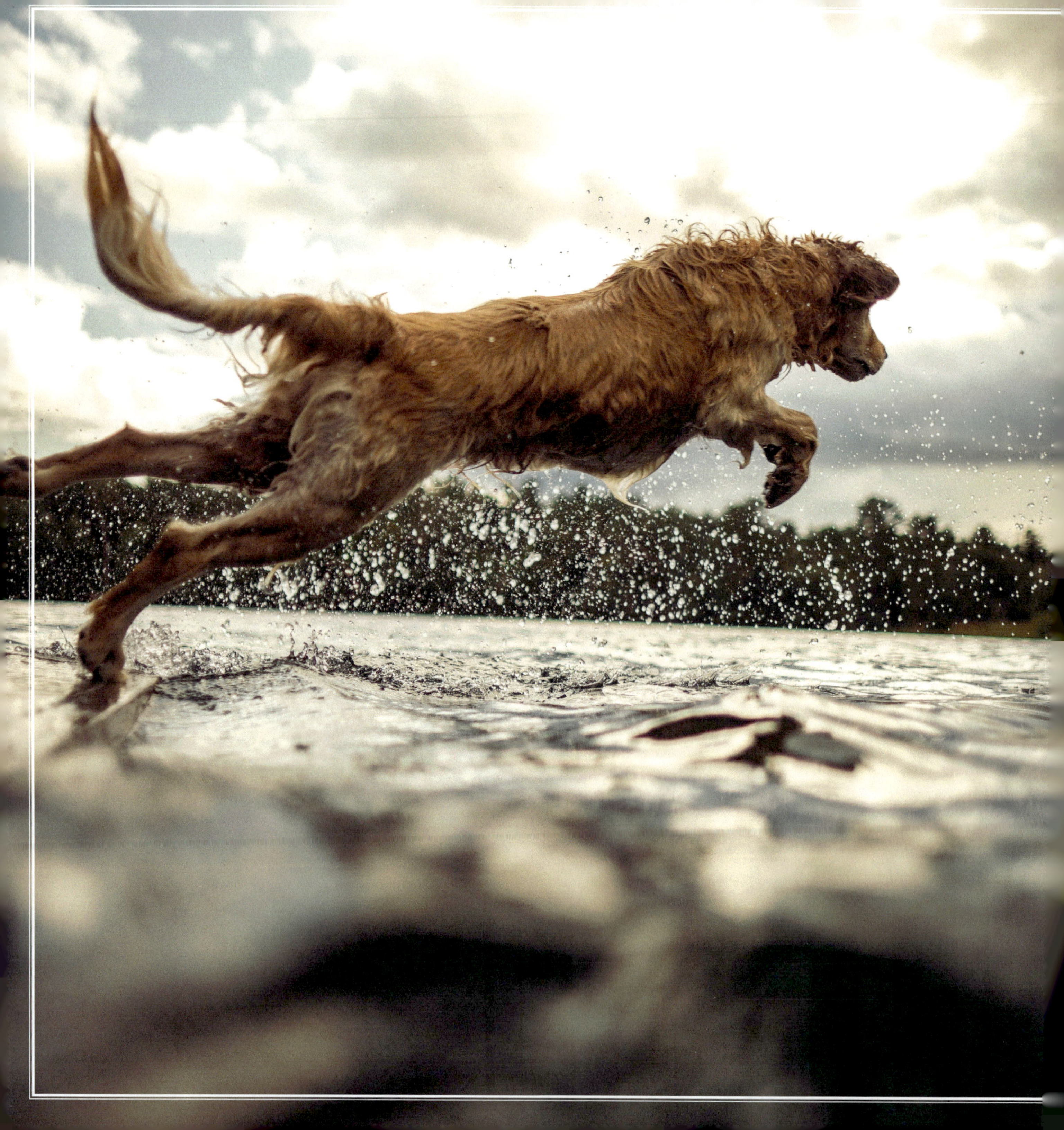

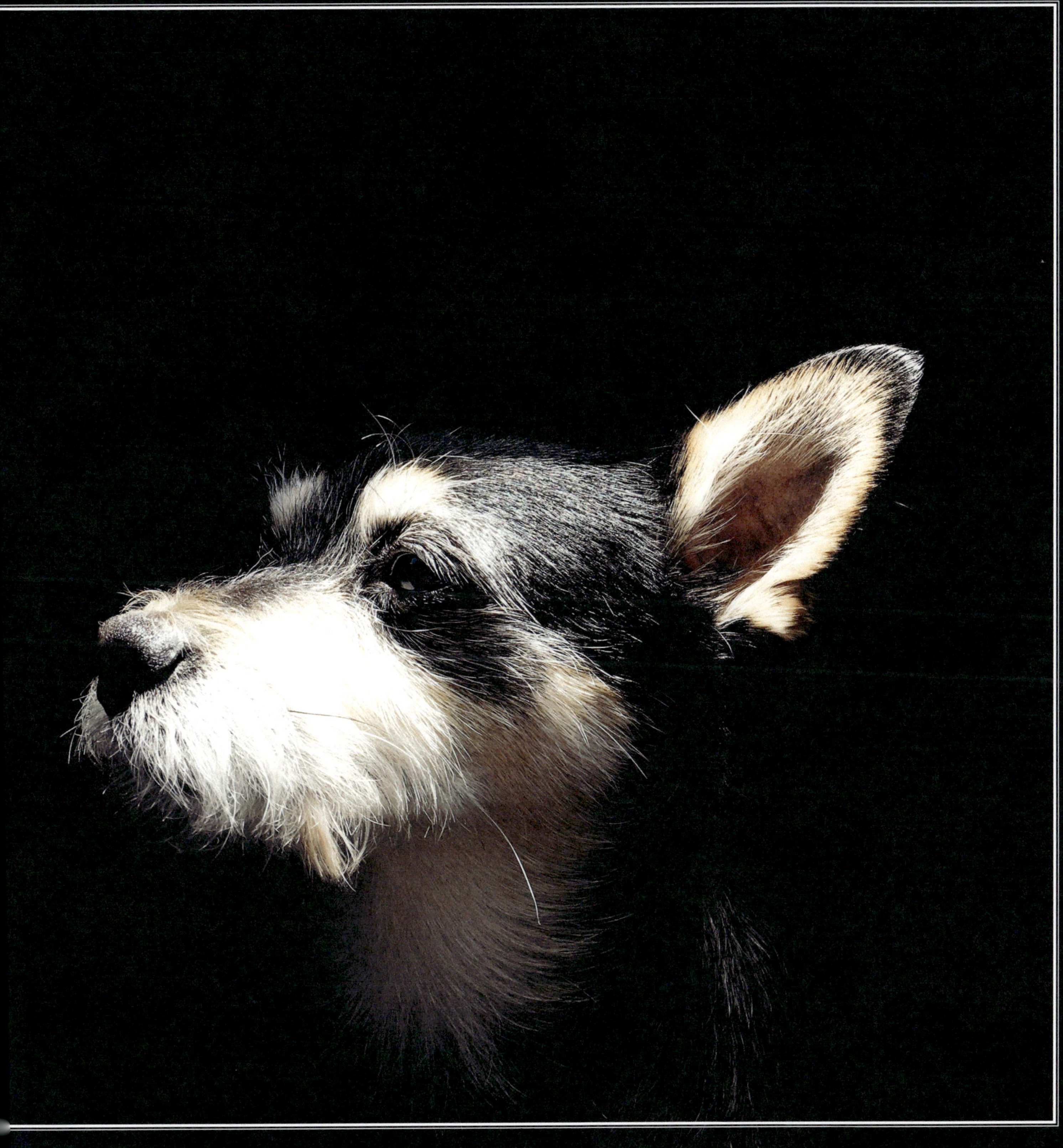

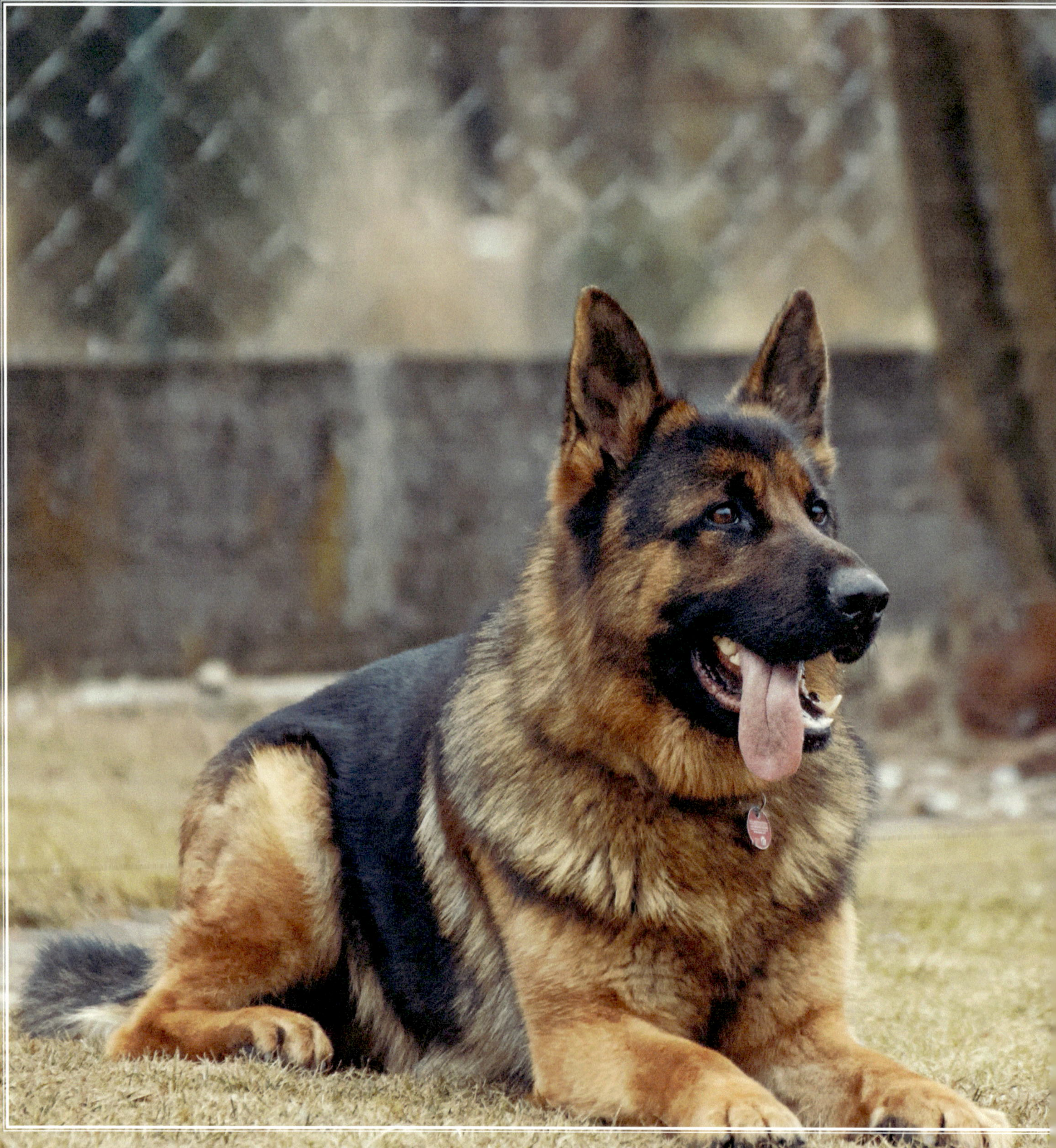

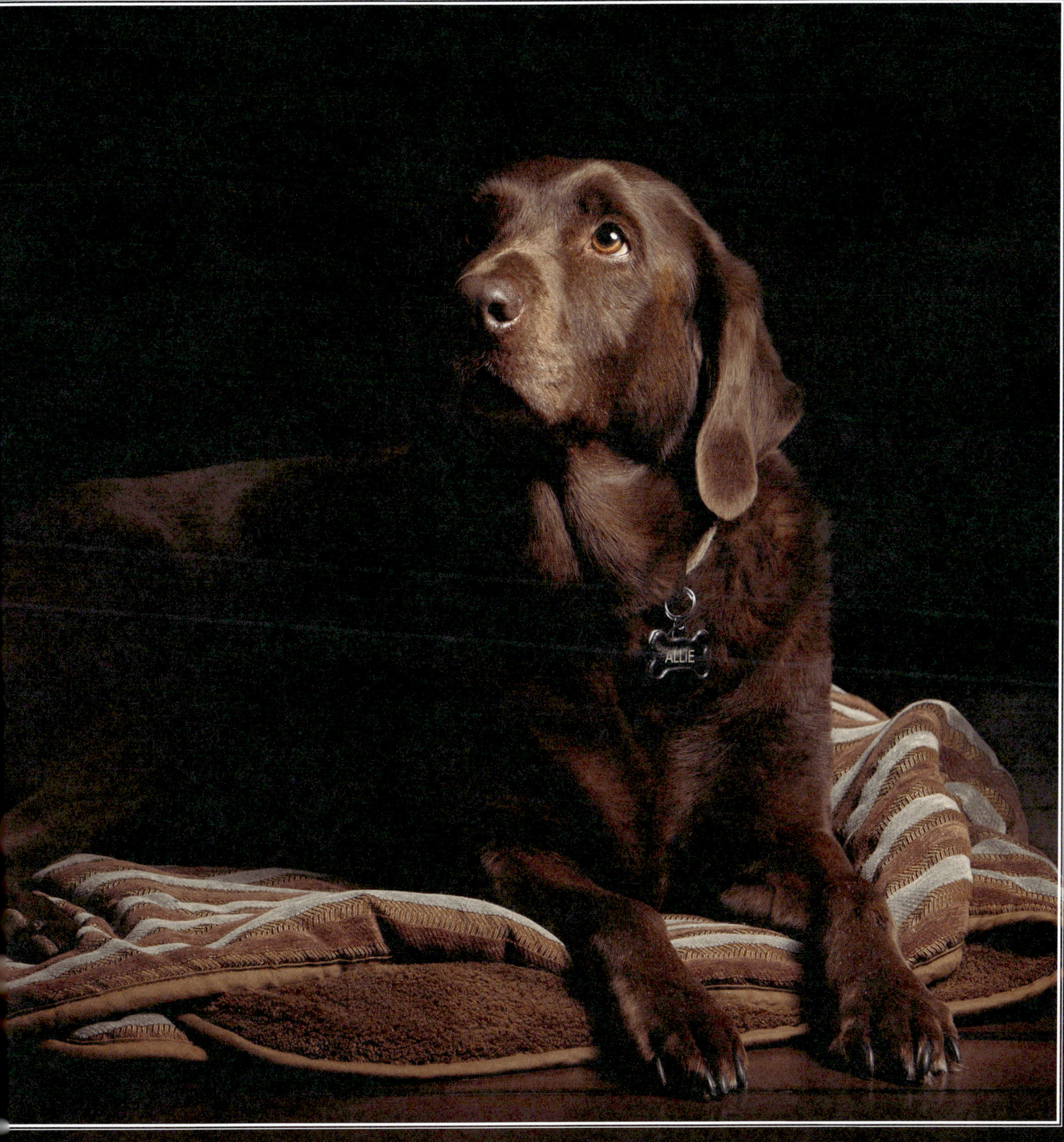
ALLIE

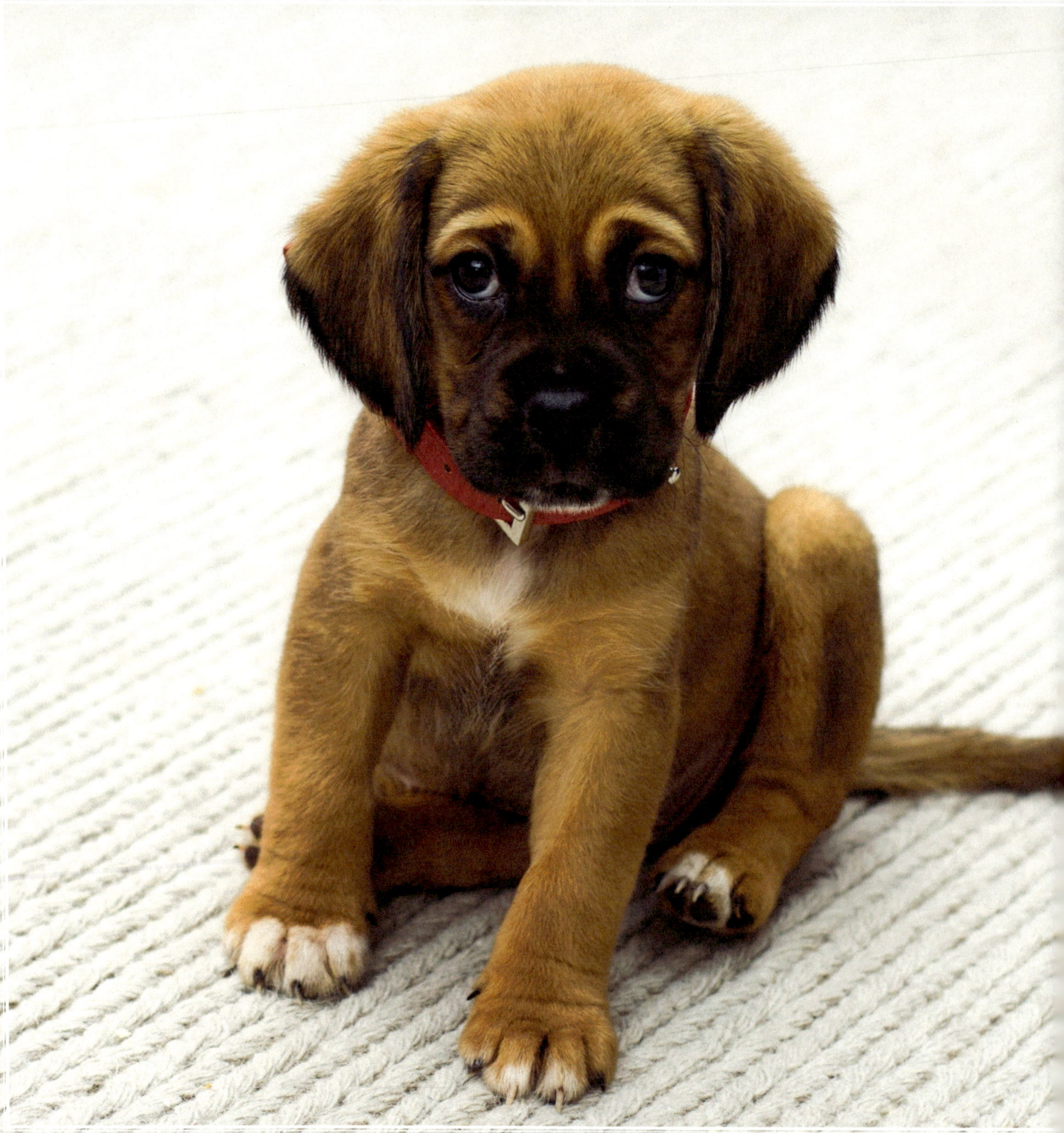

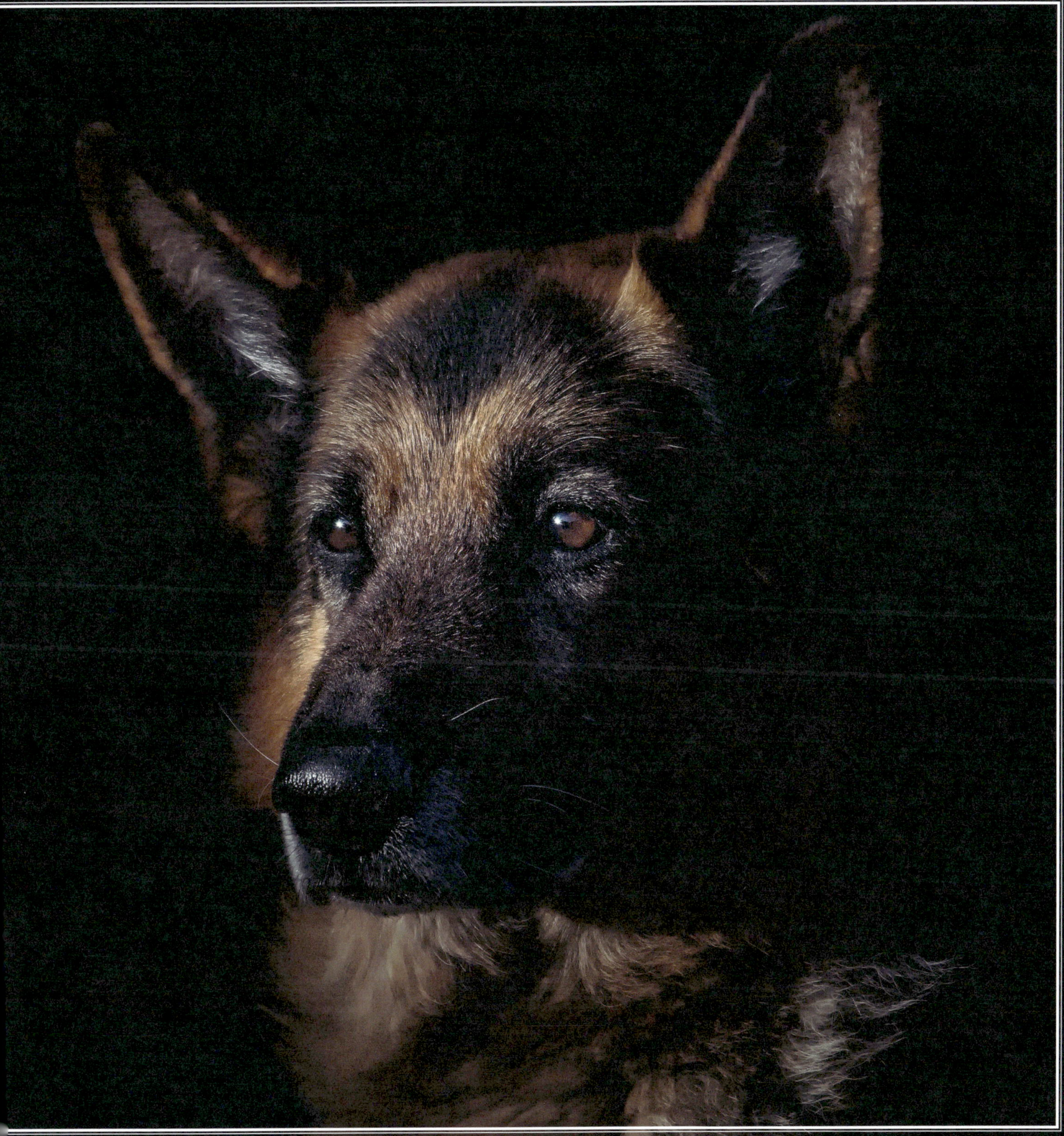

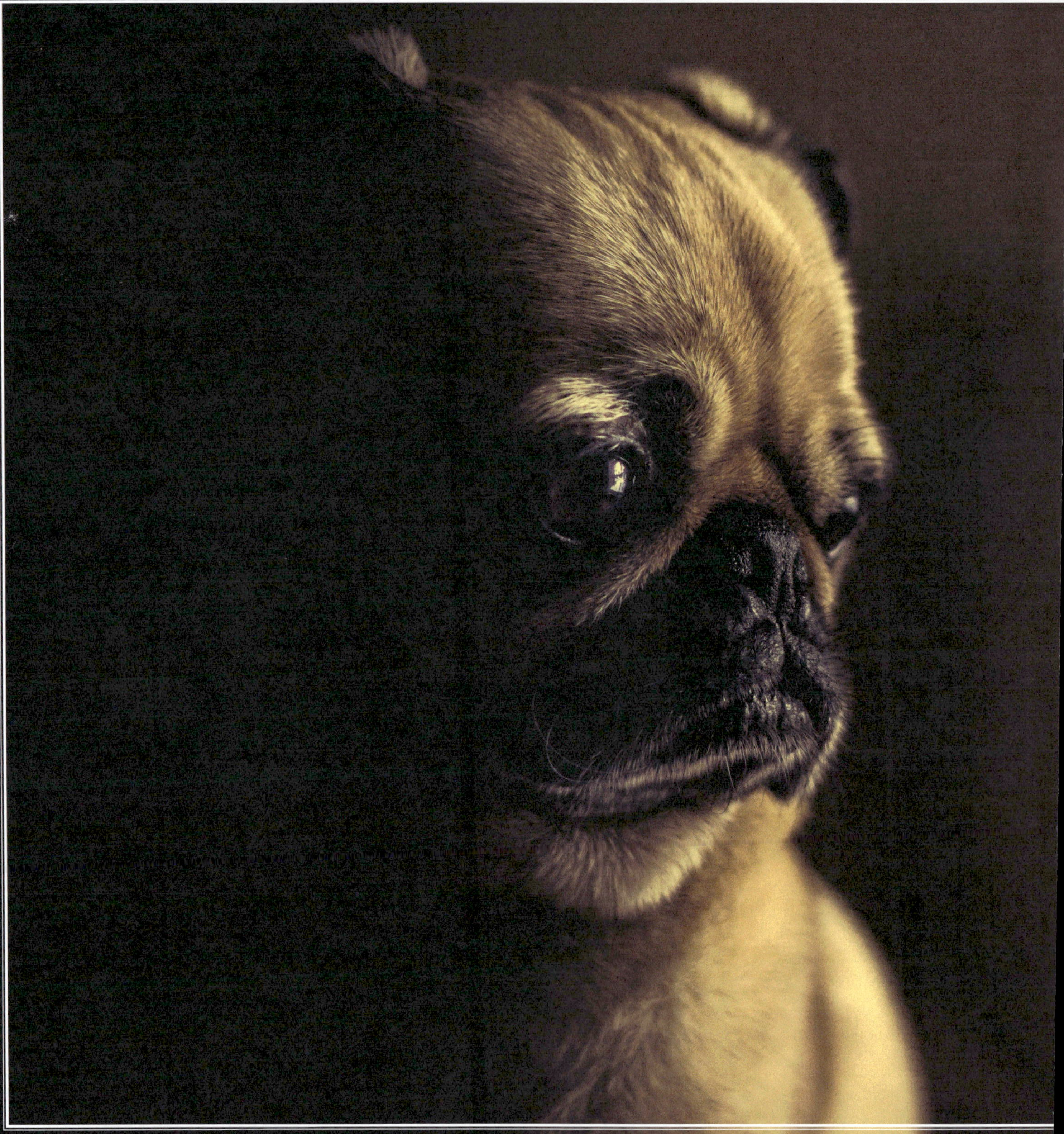

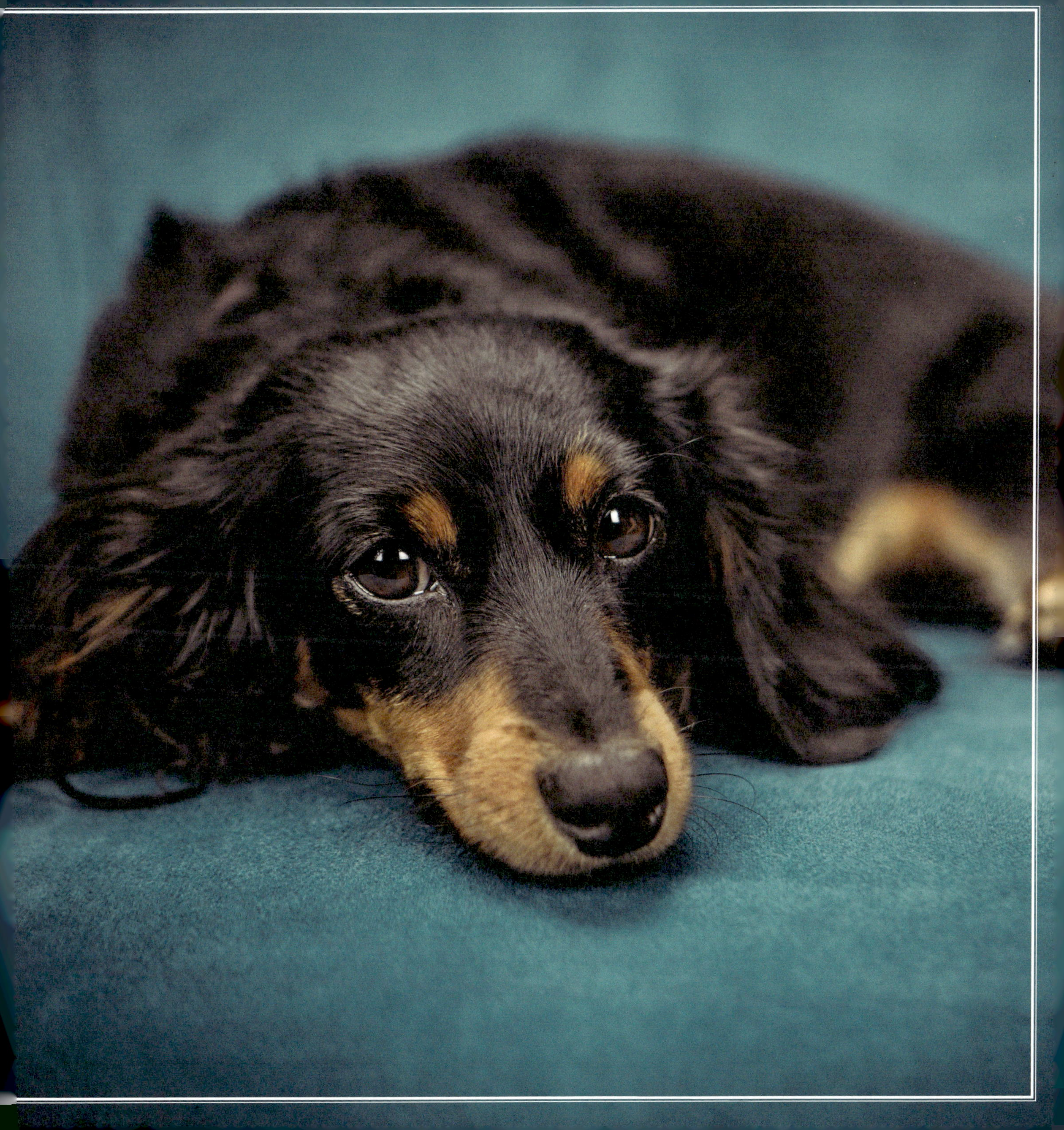

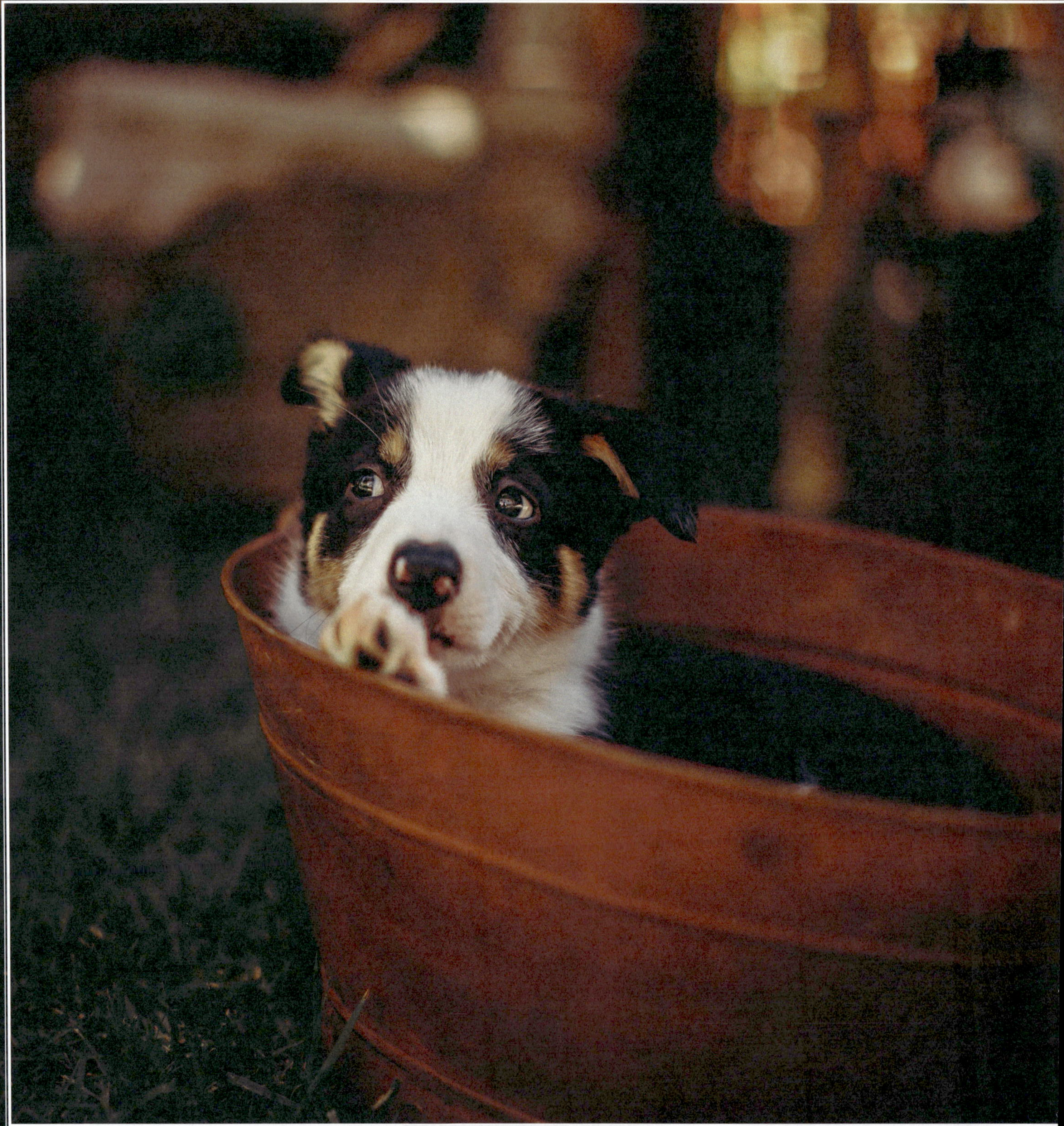

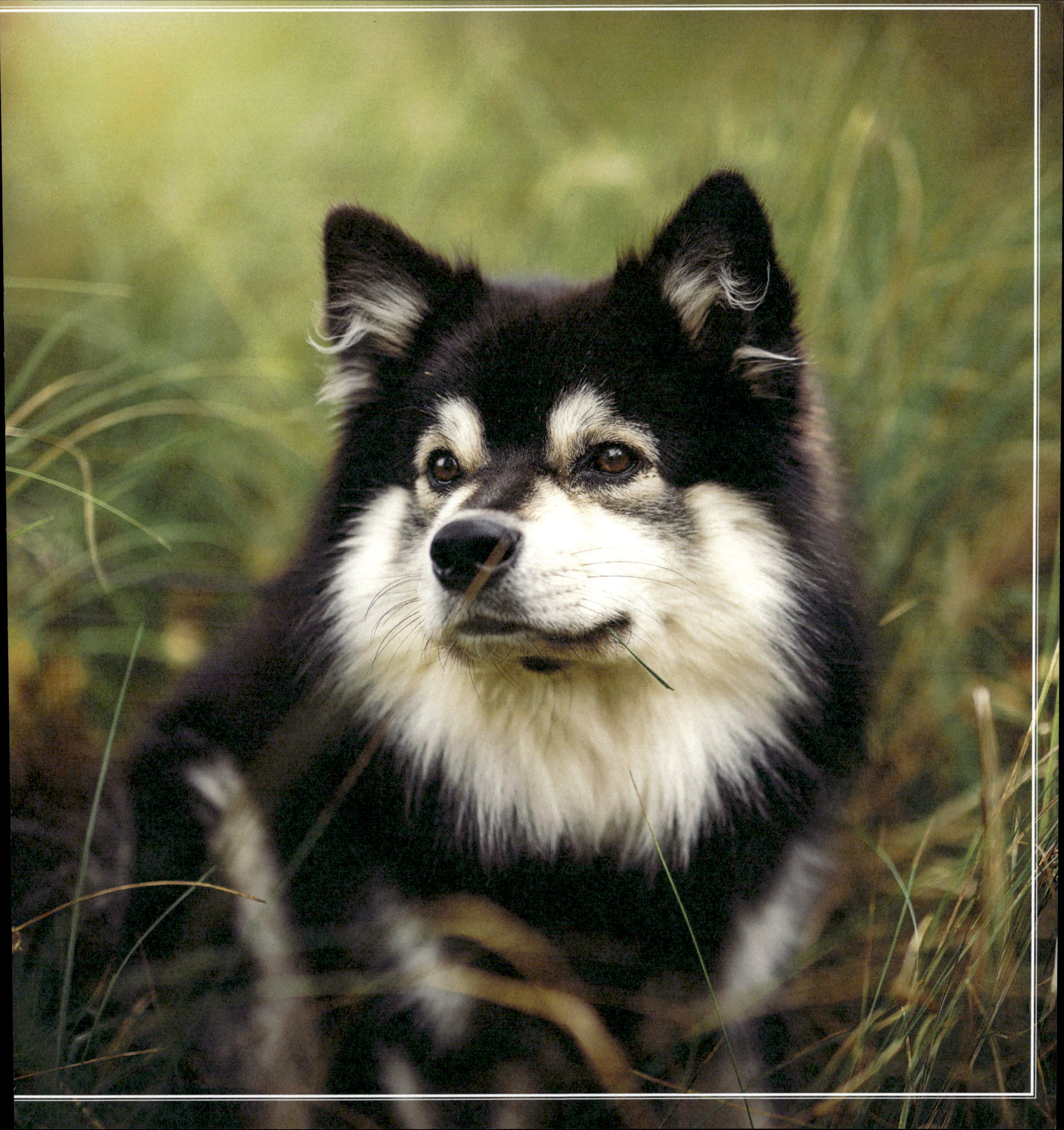

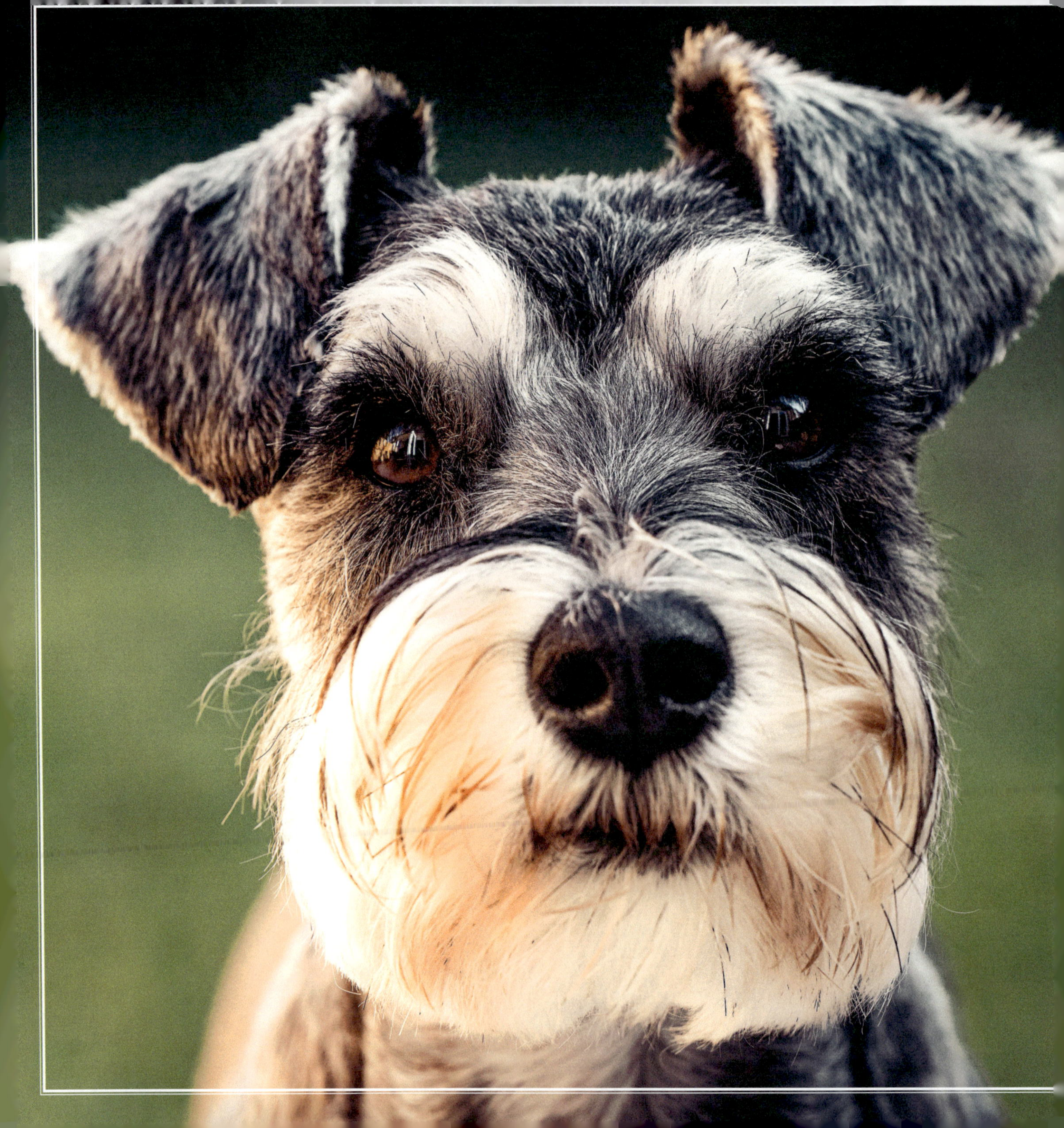

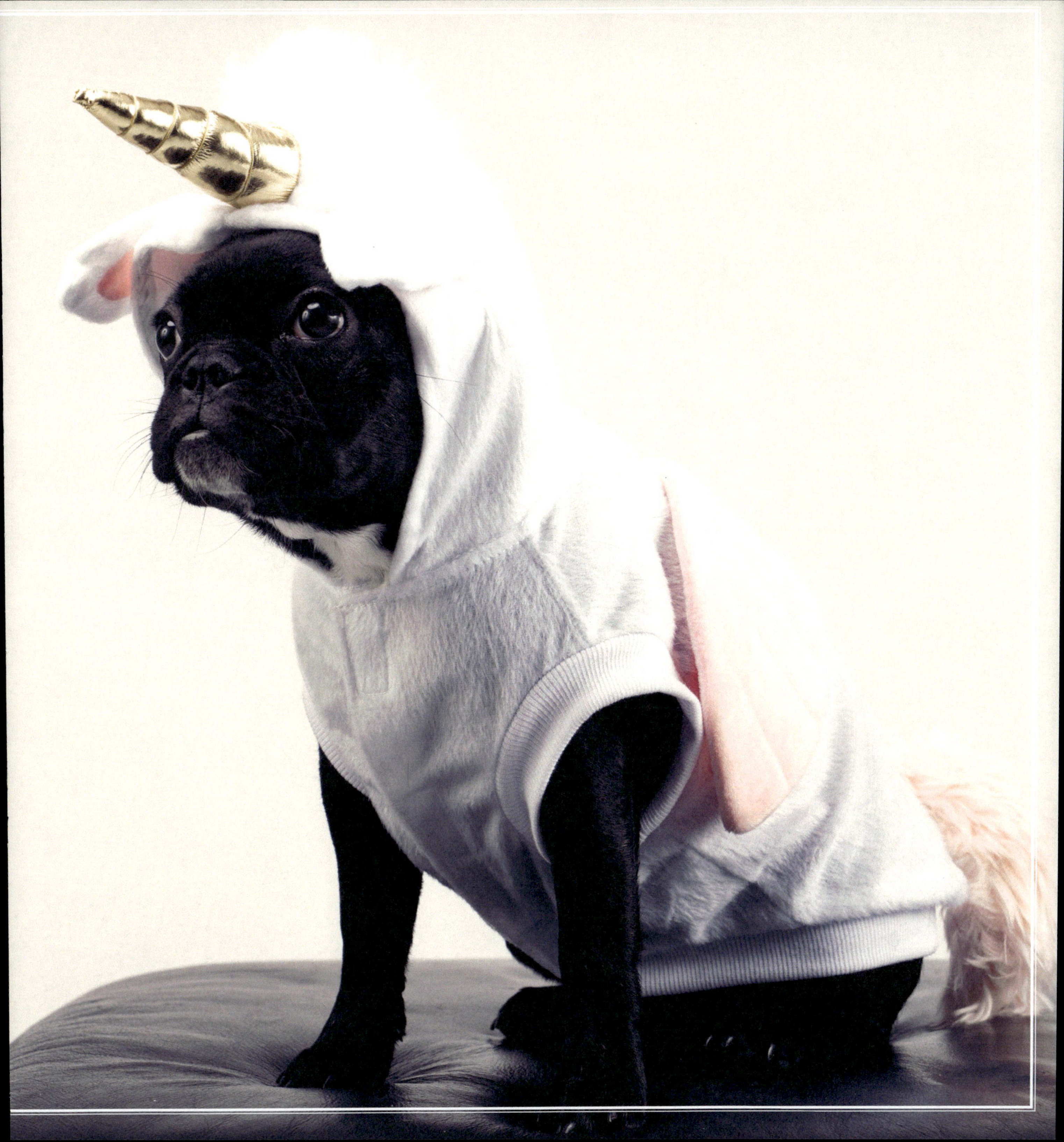

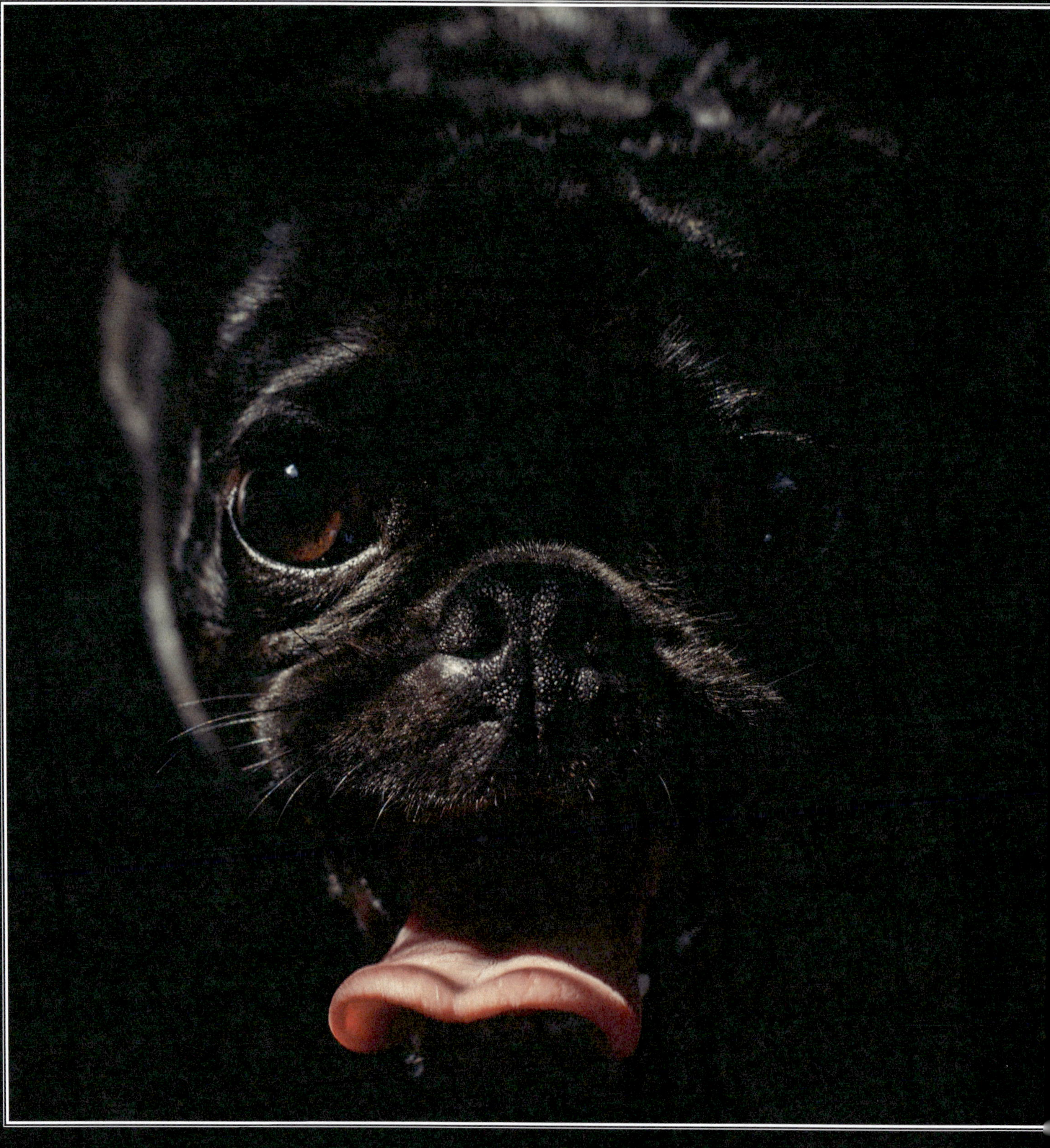

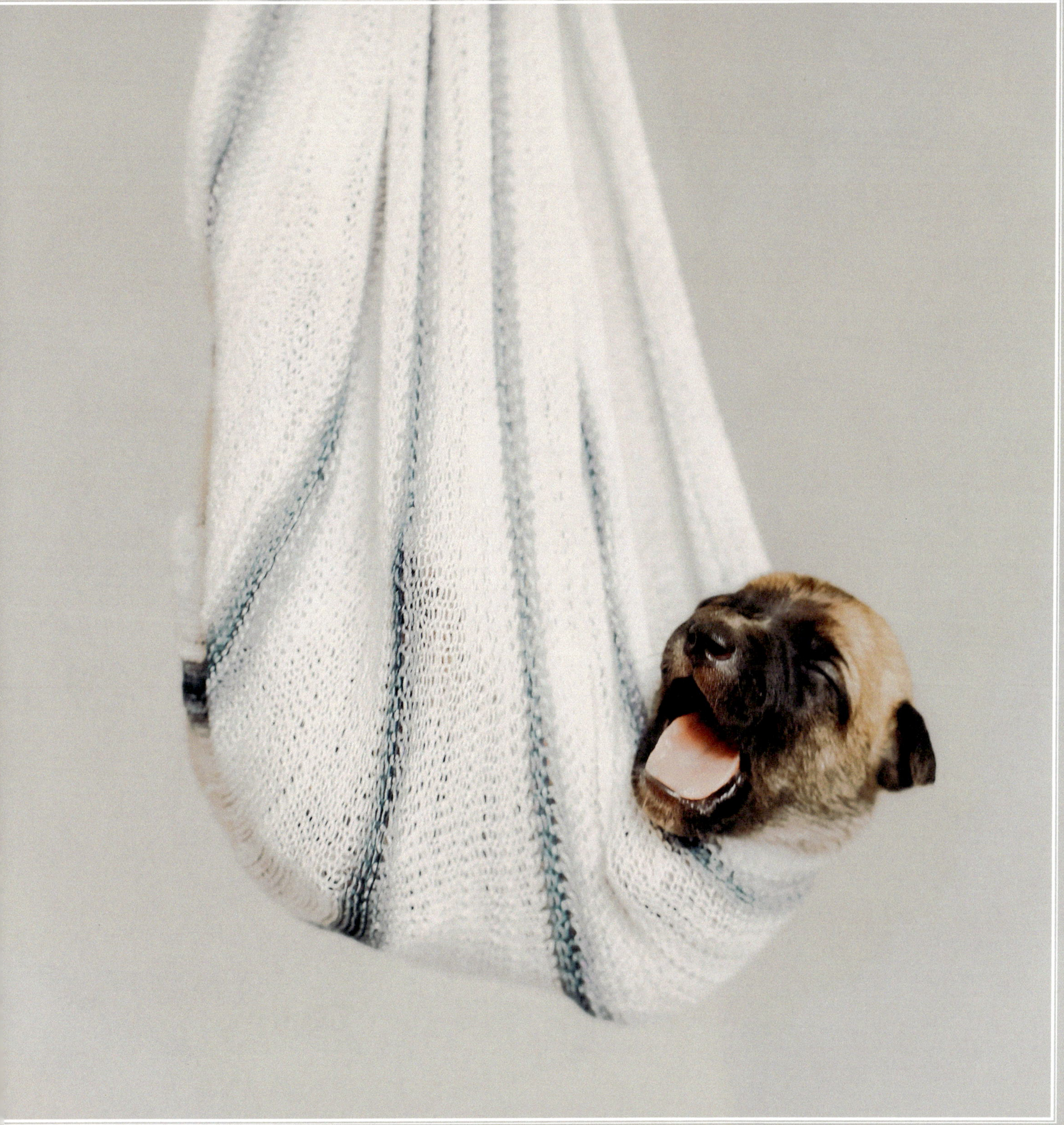

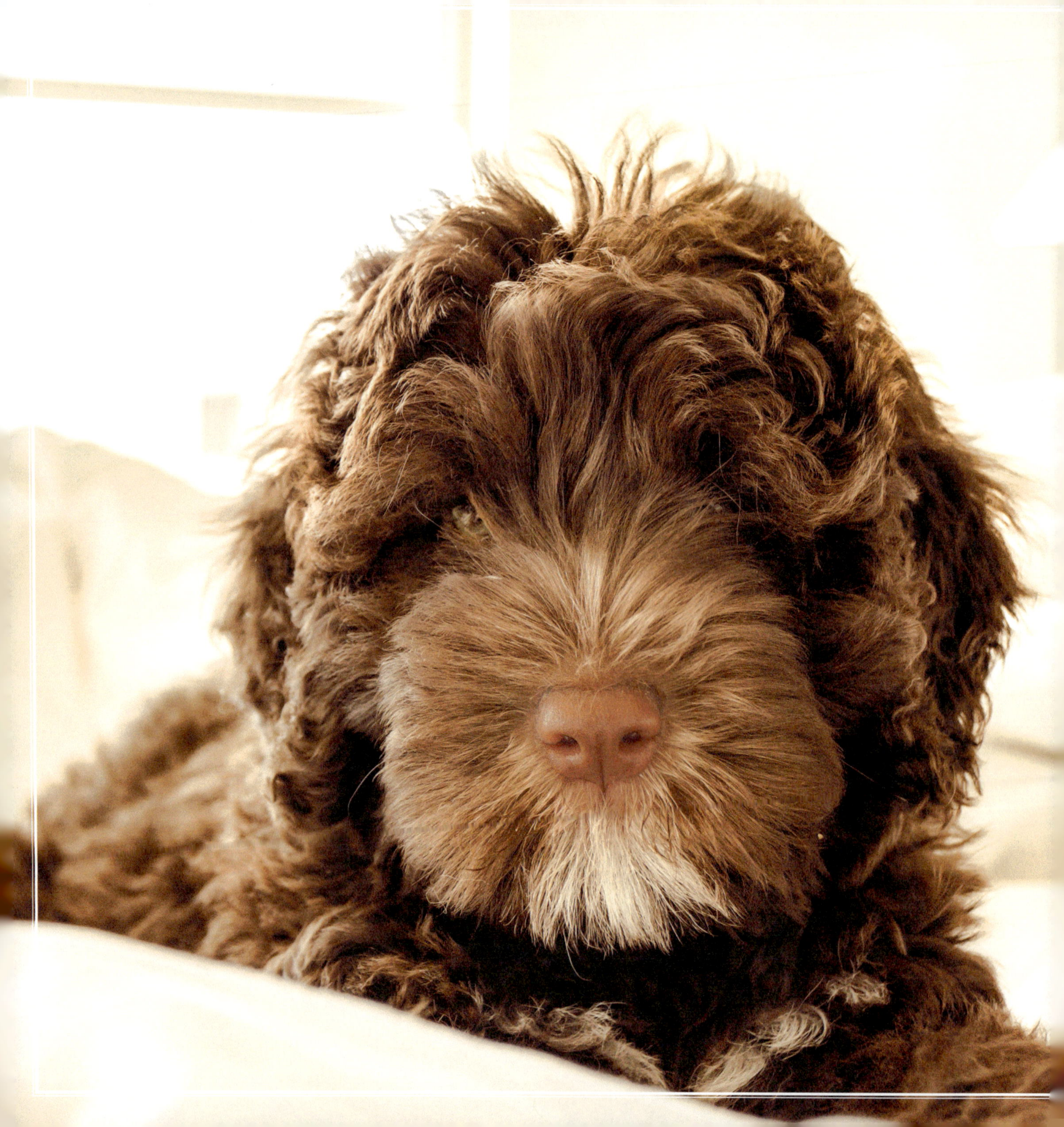

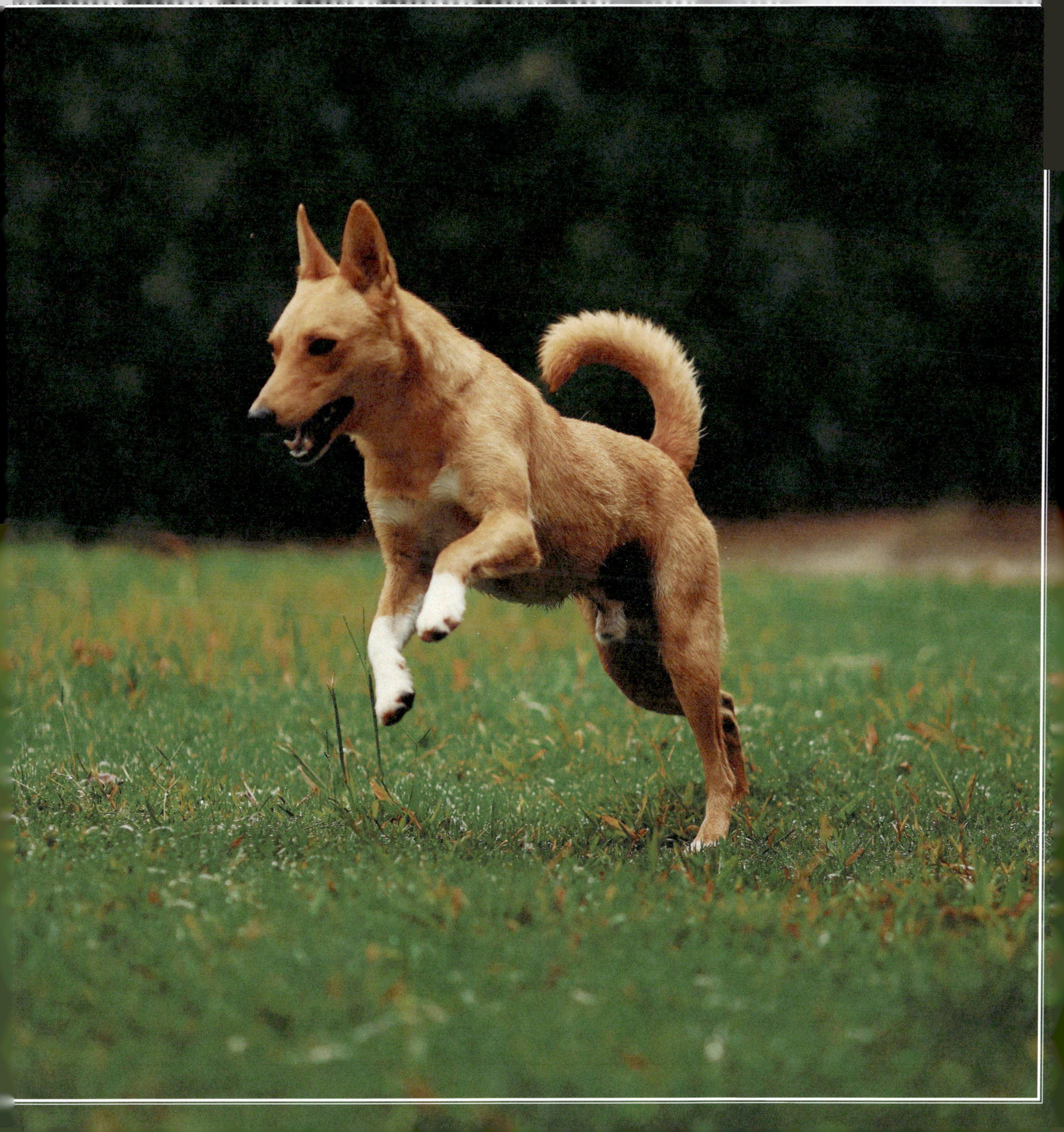

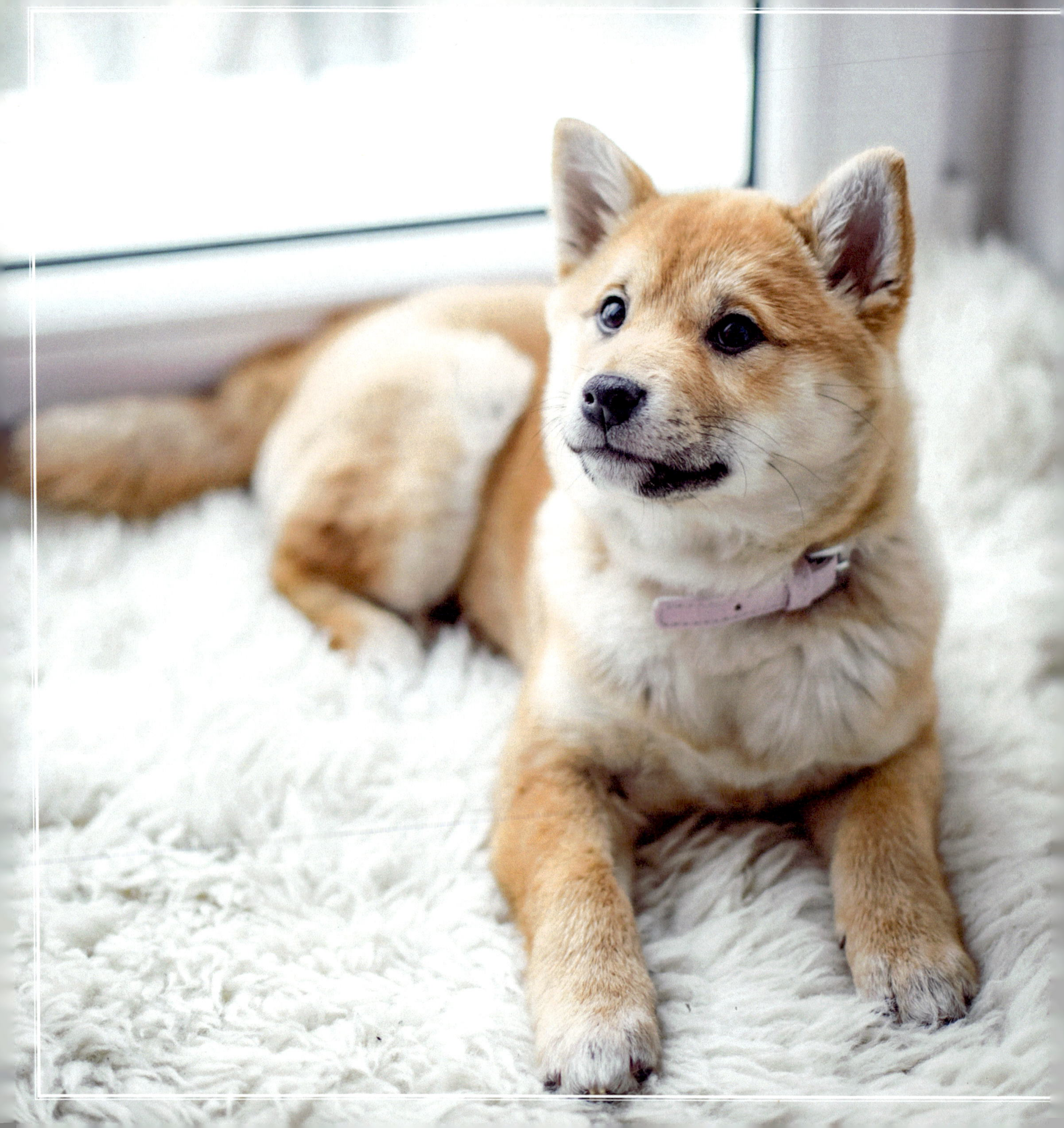

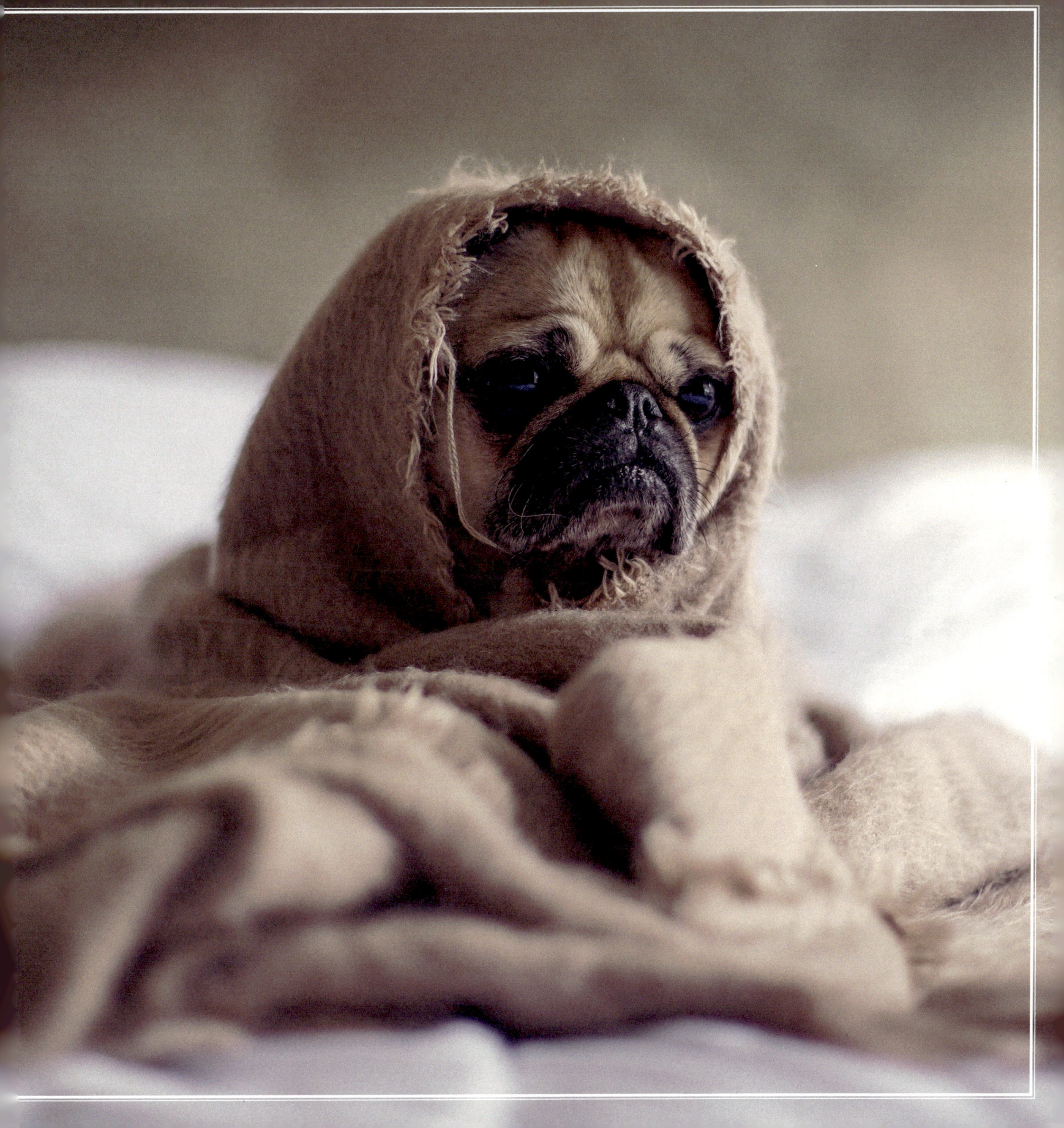

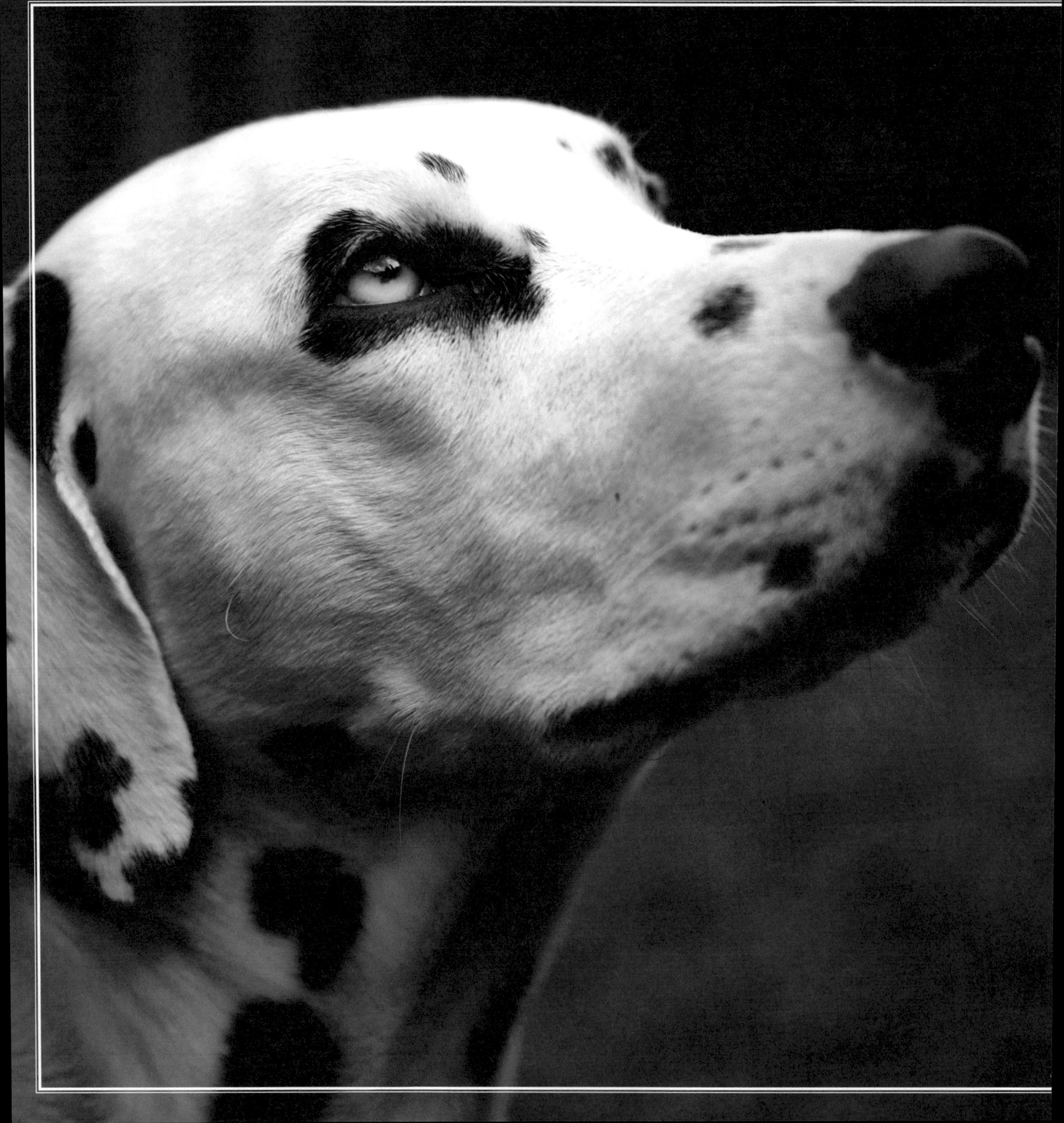

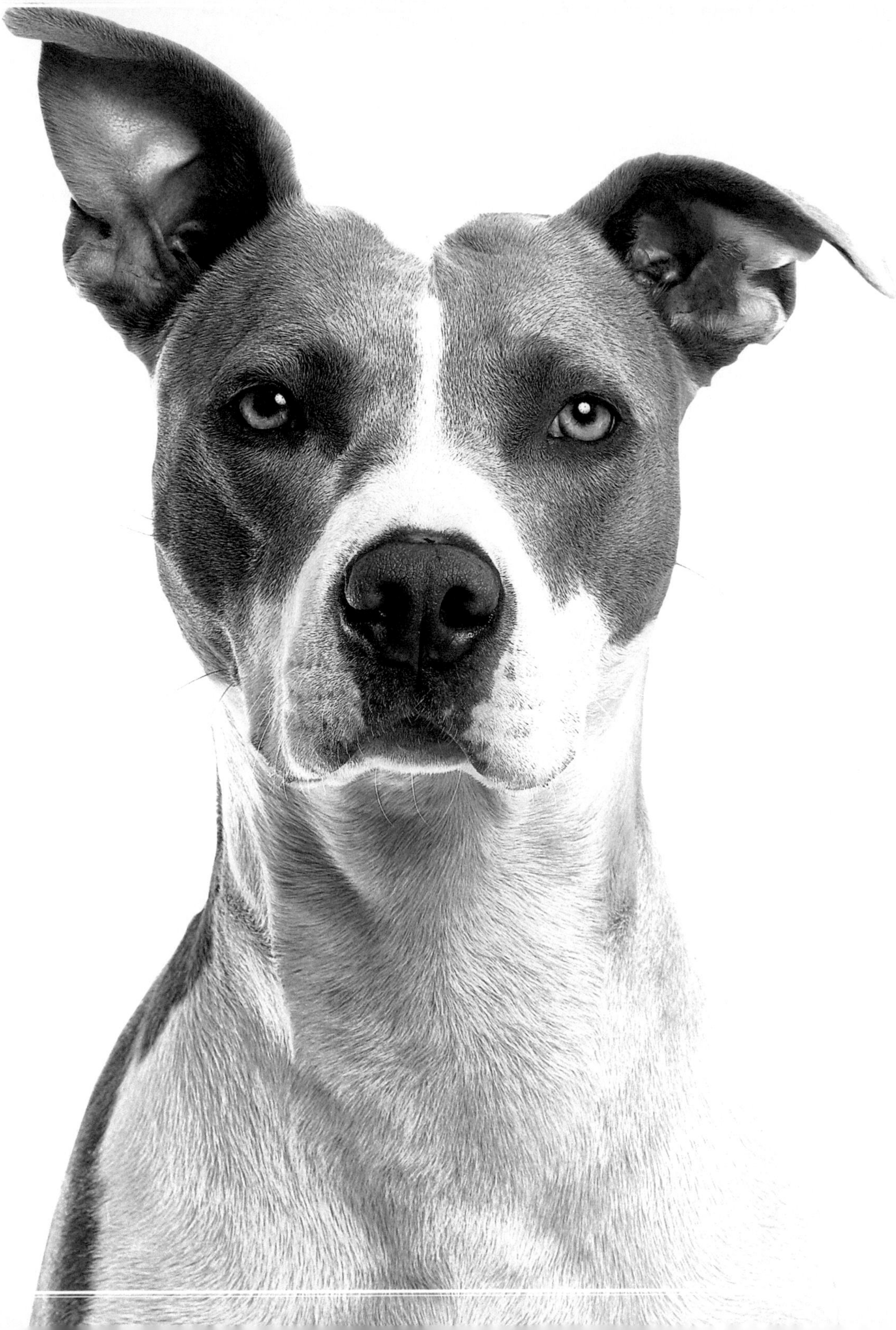

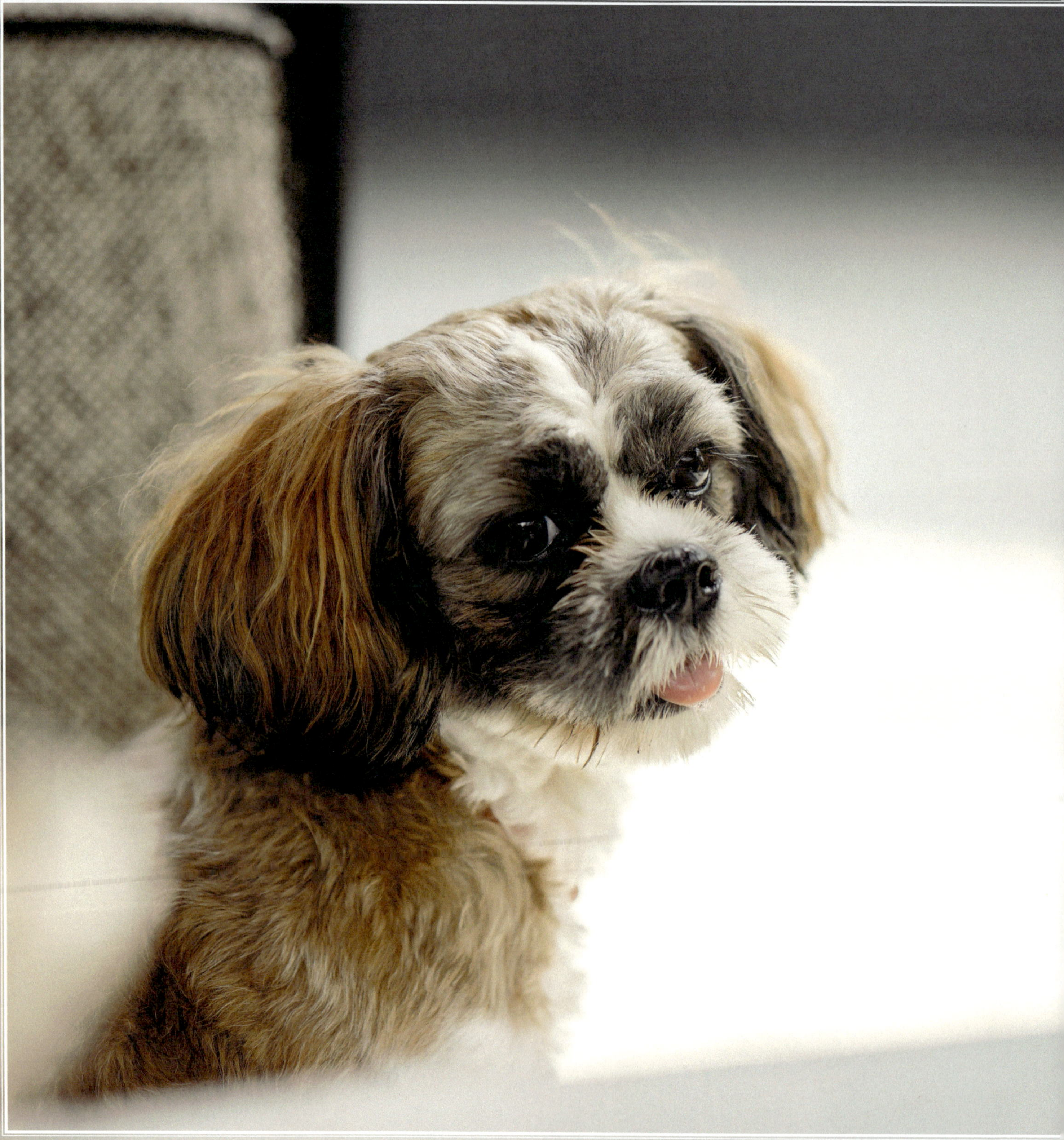

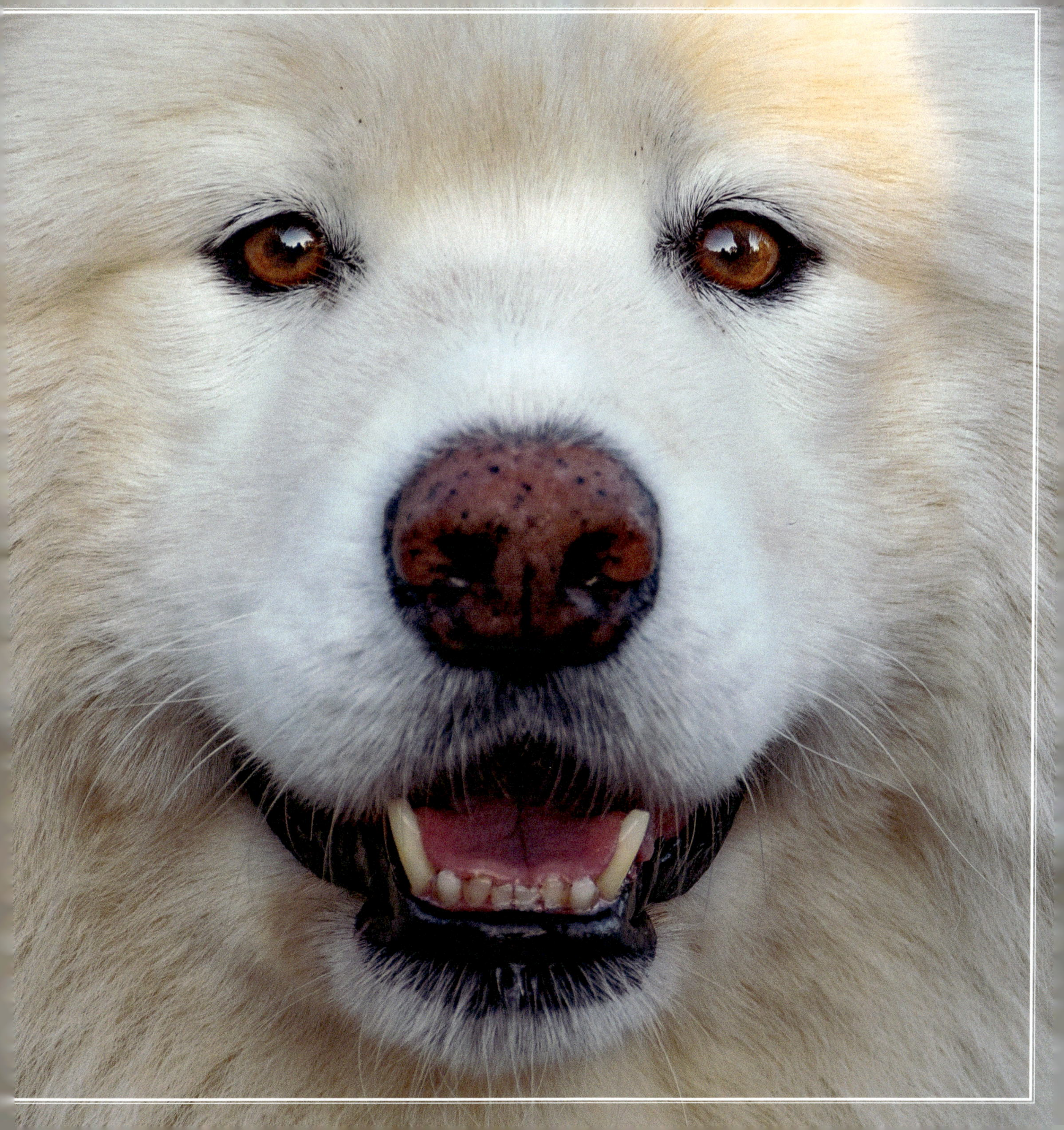

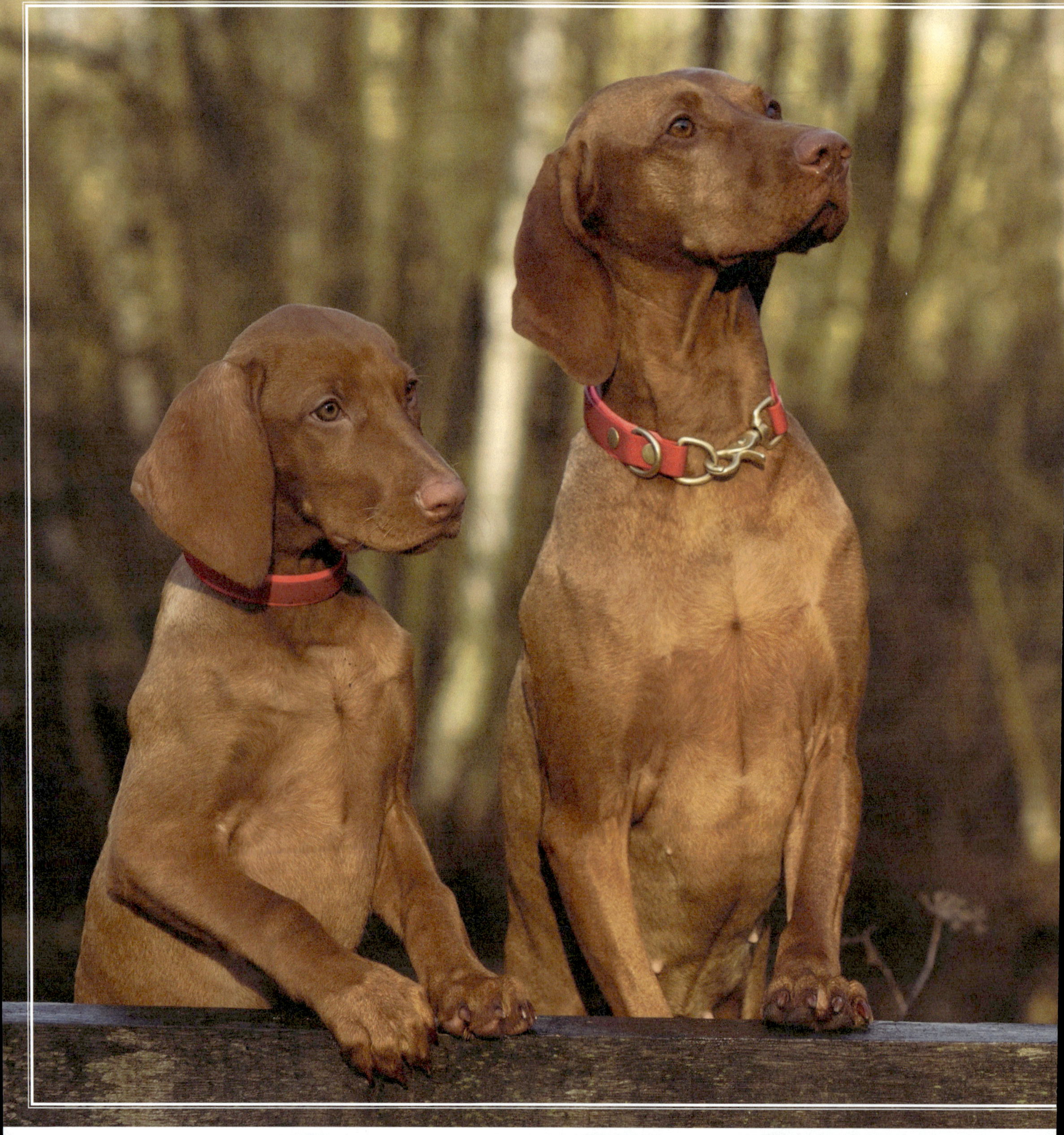

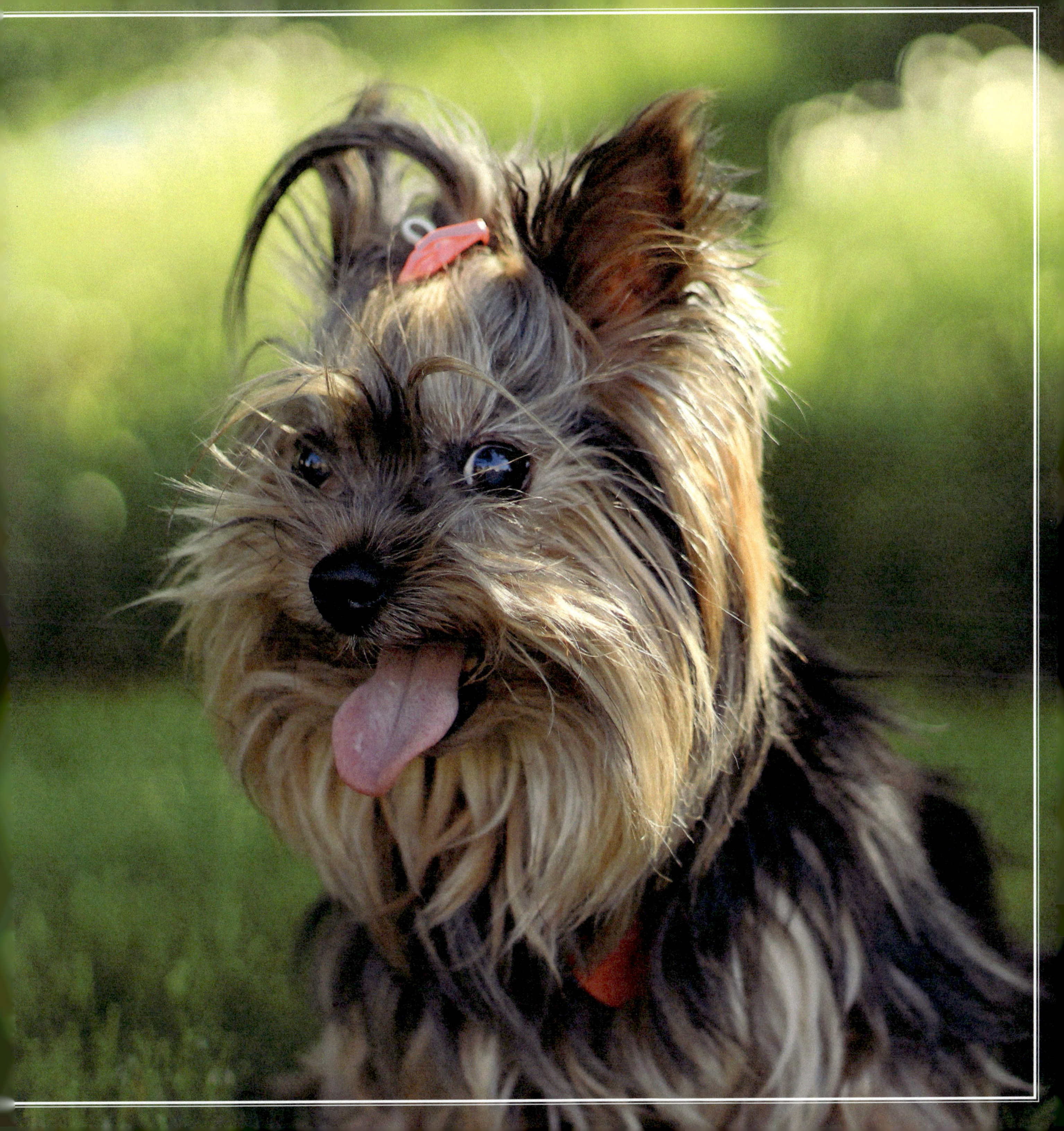

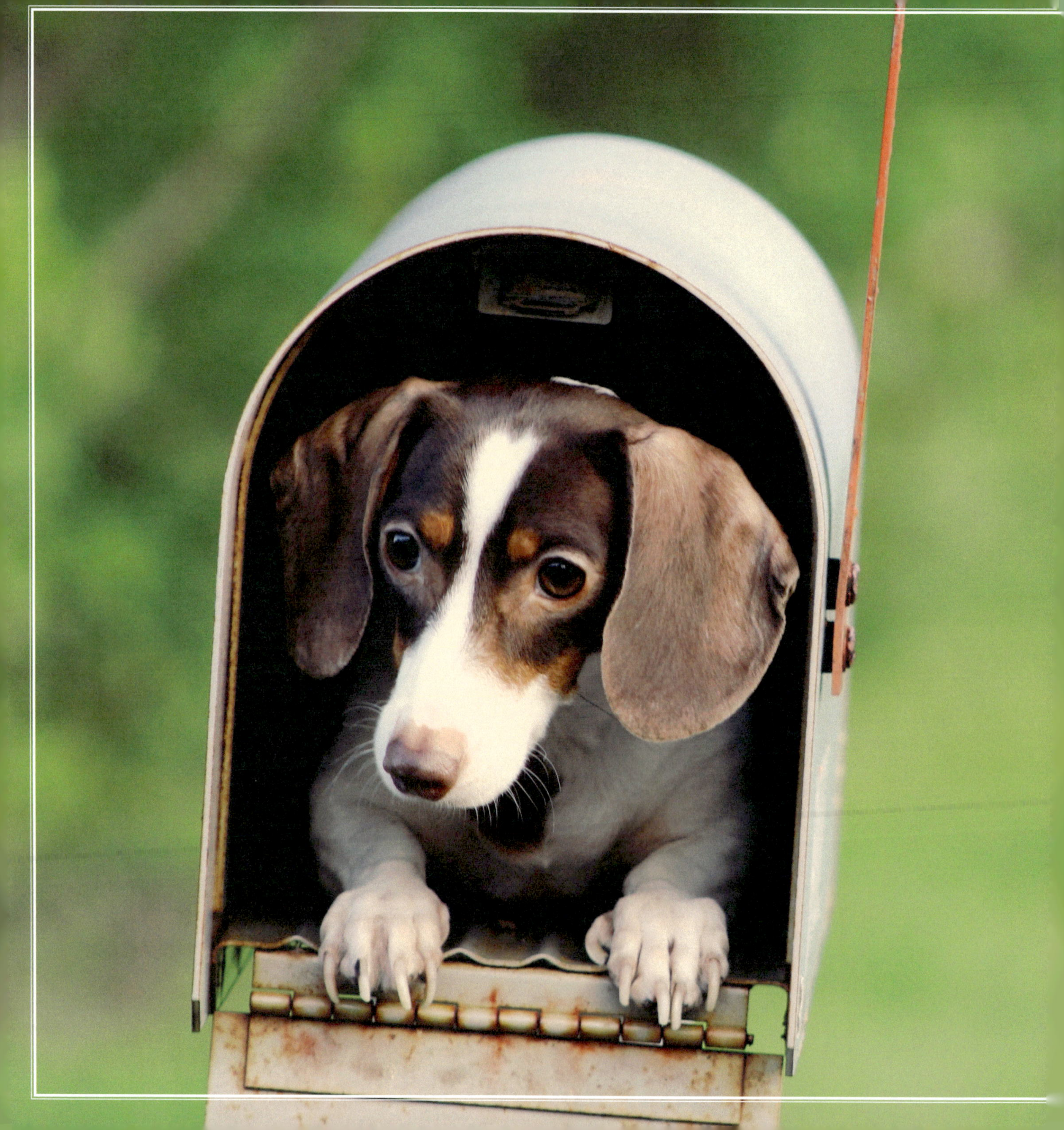

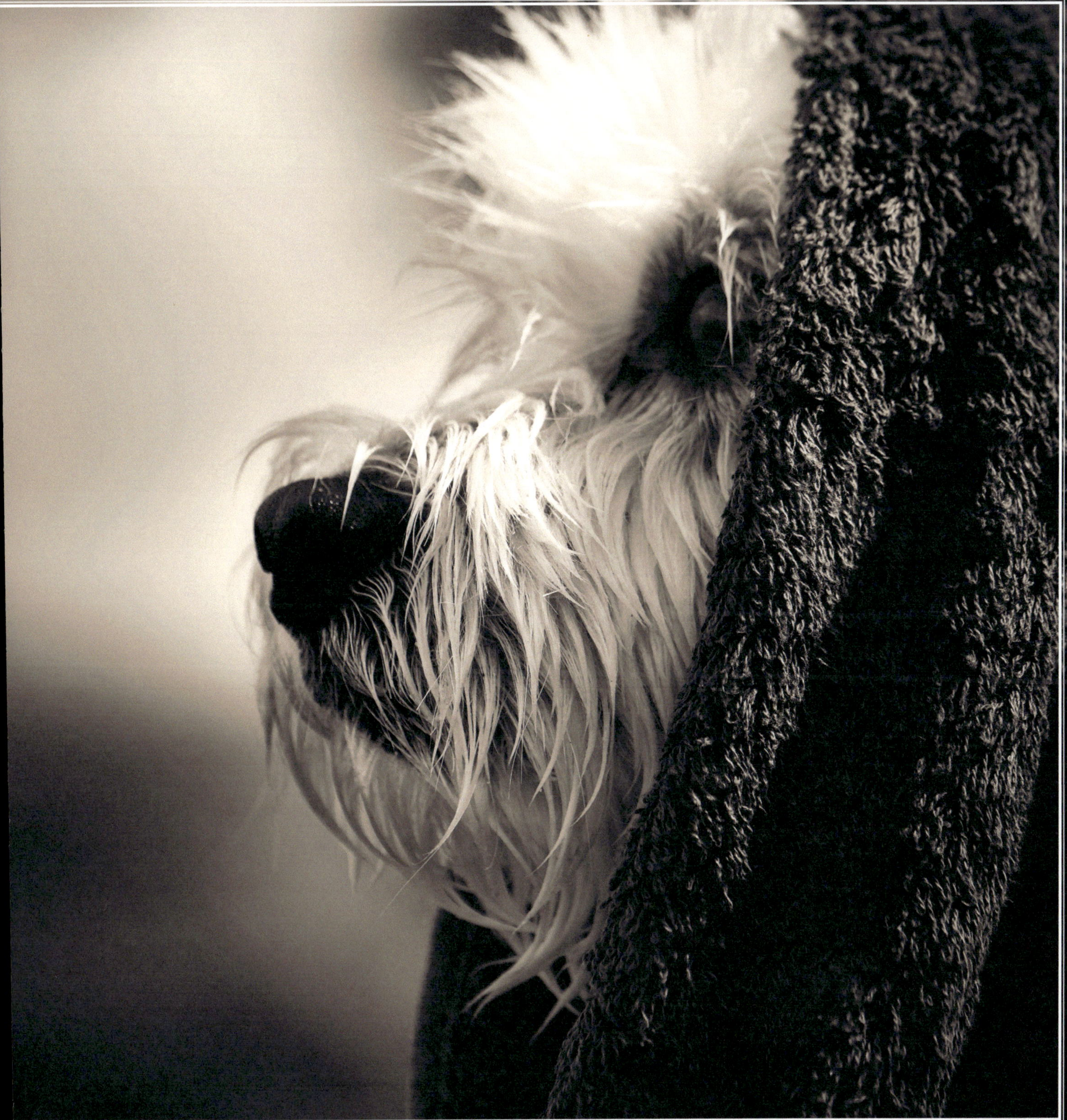

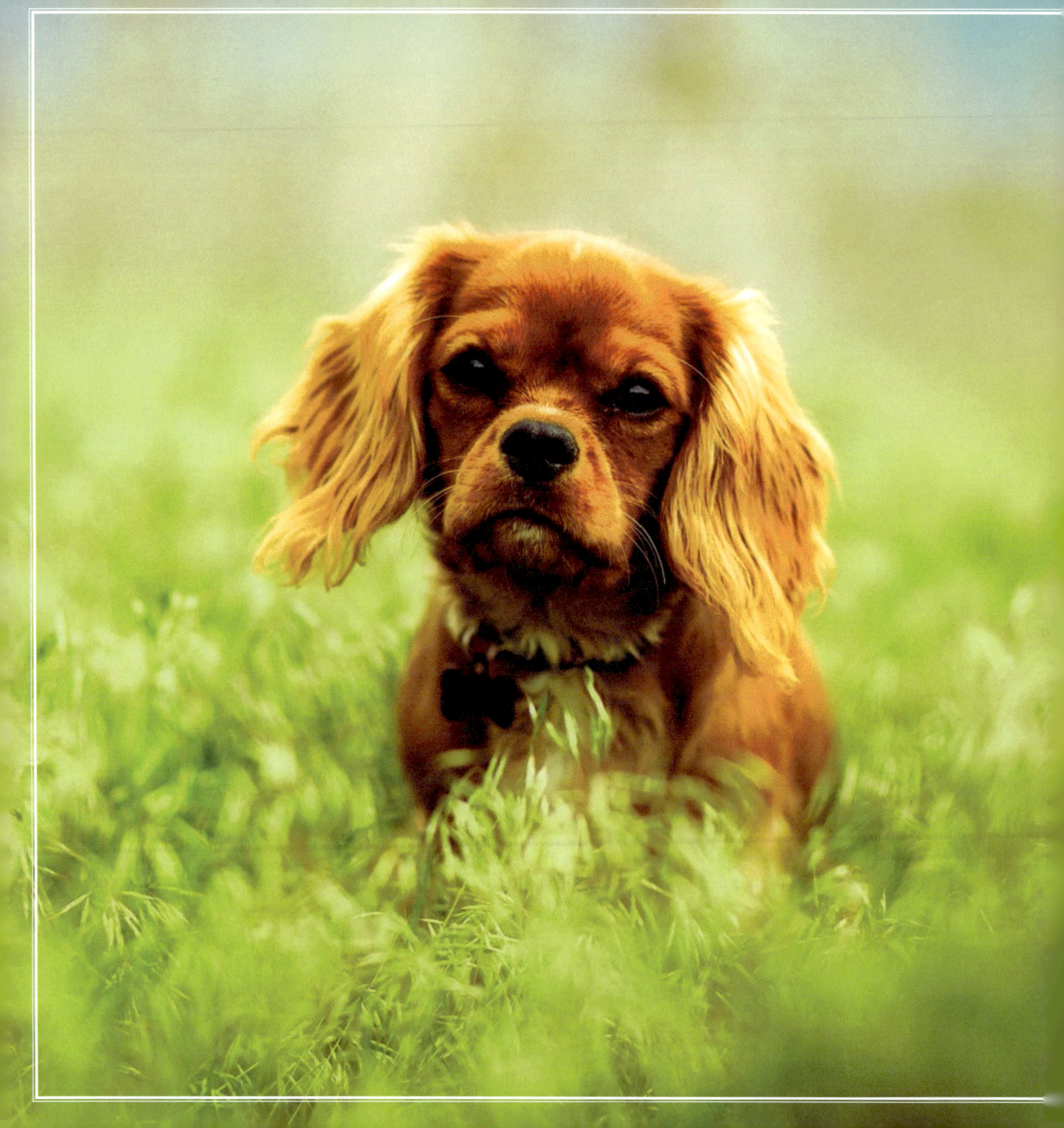

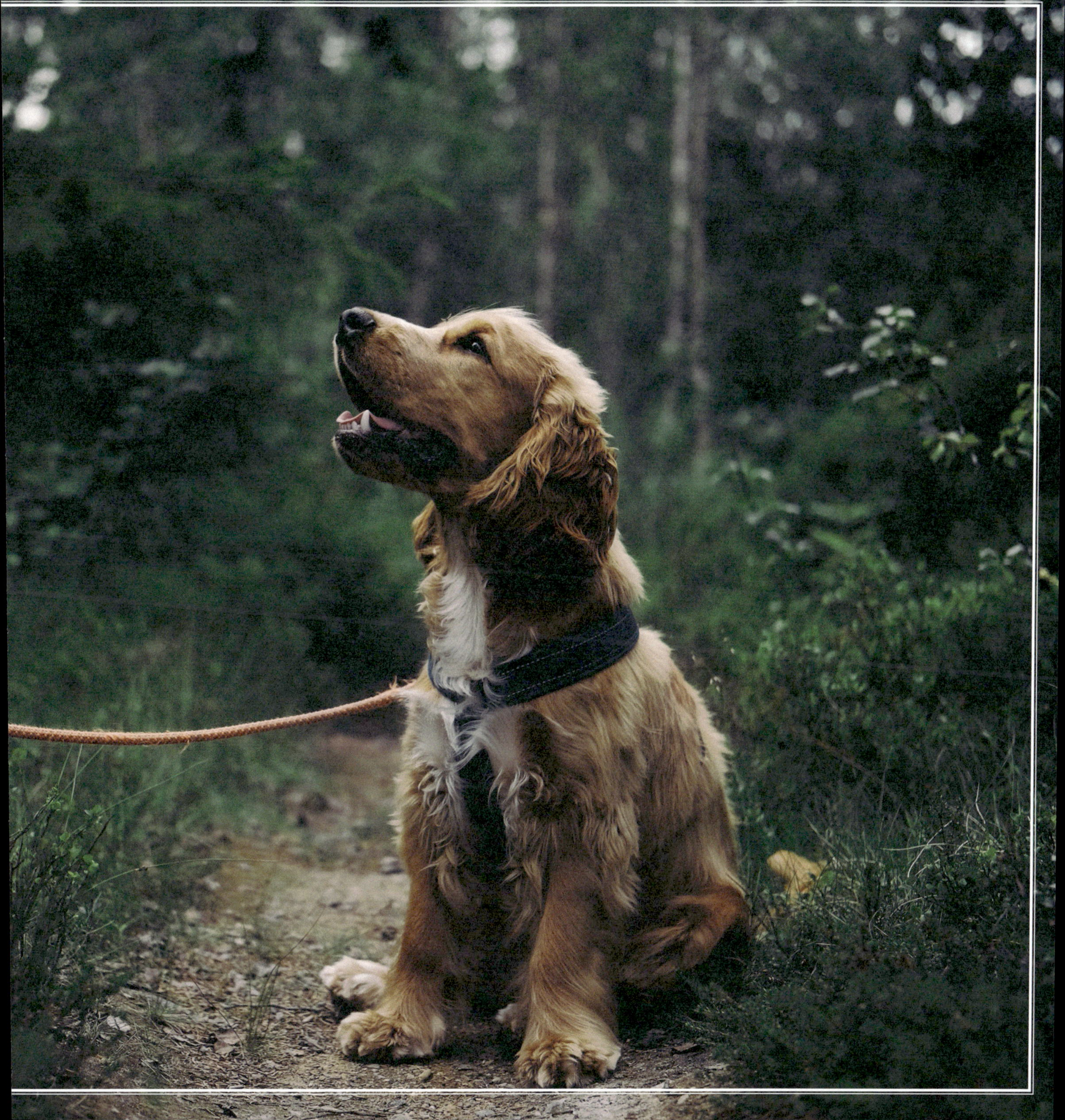

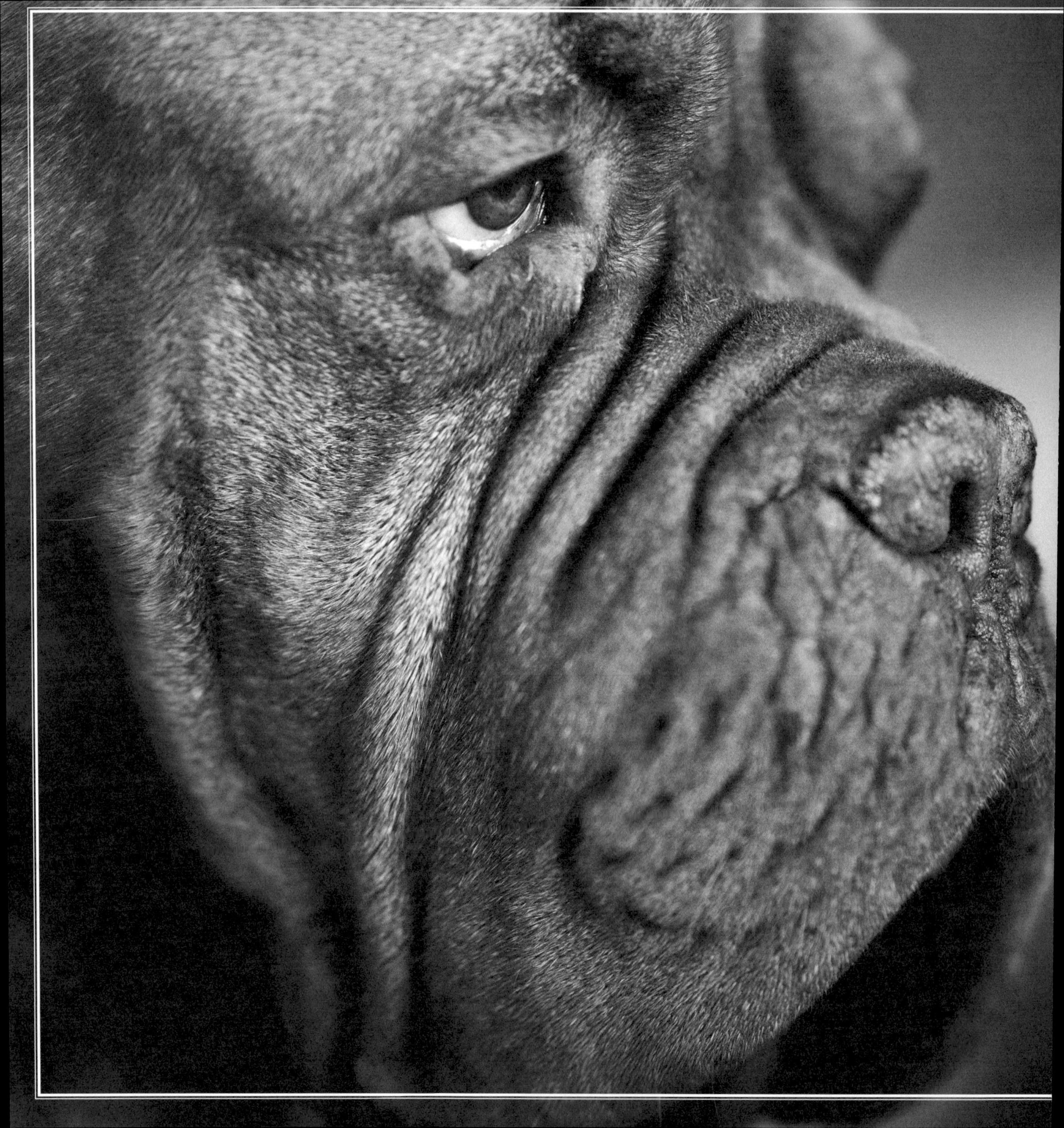

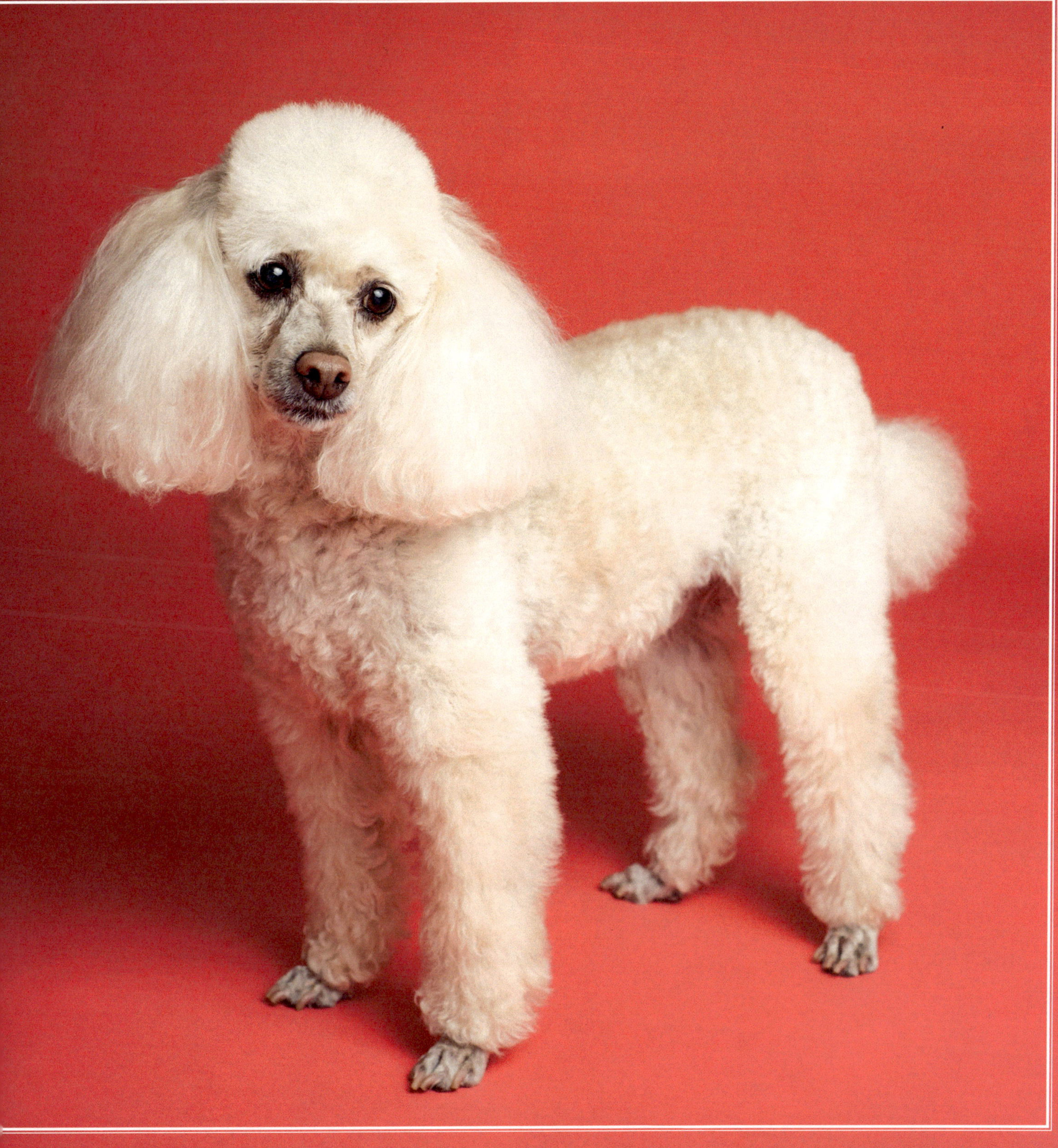

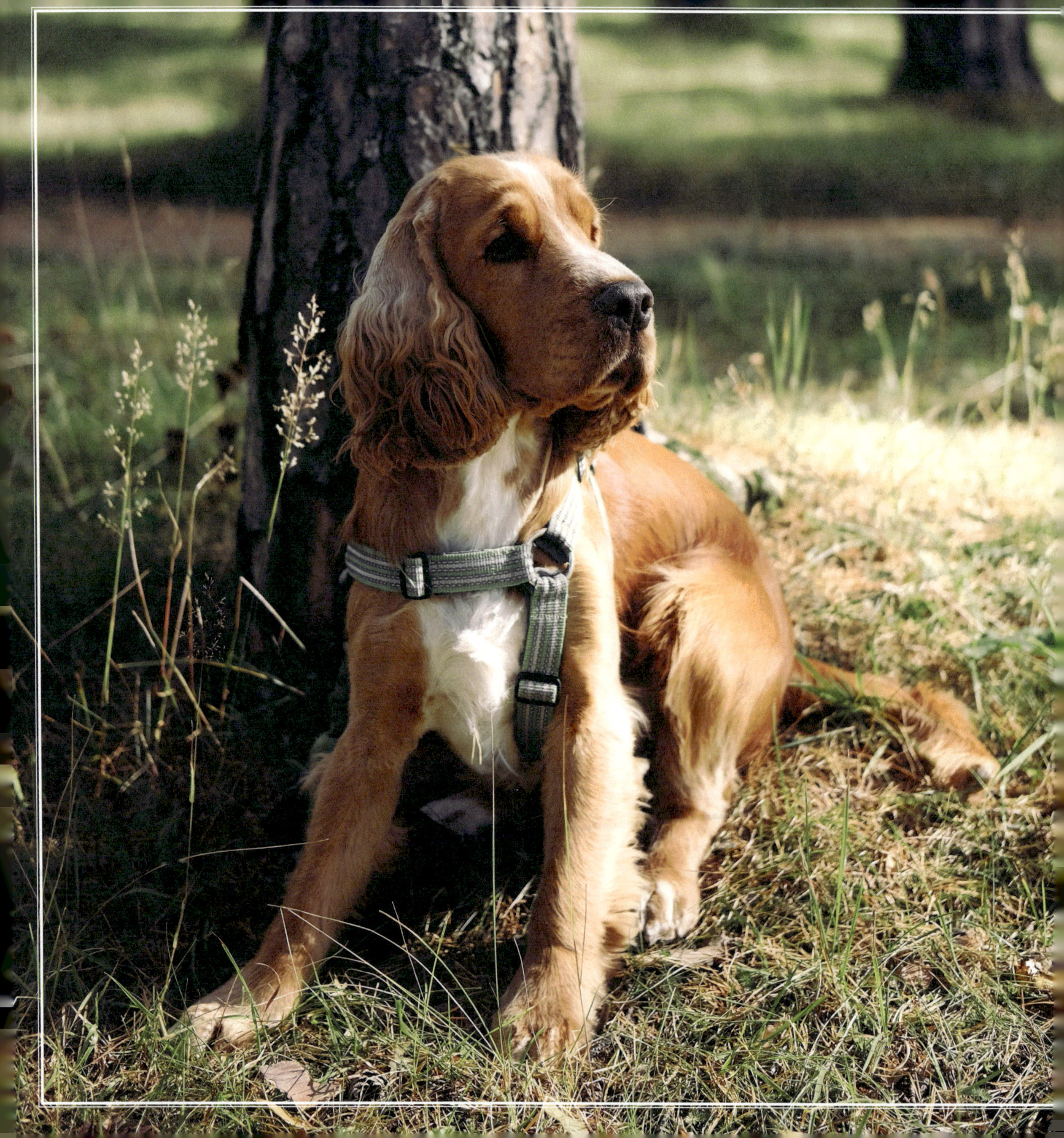

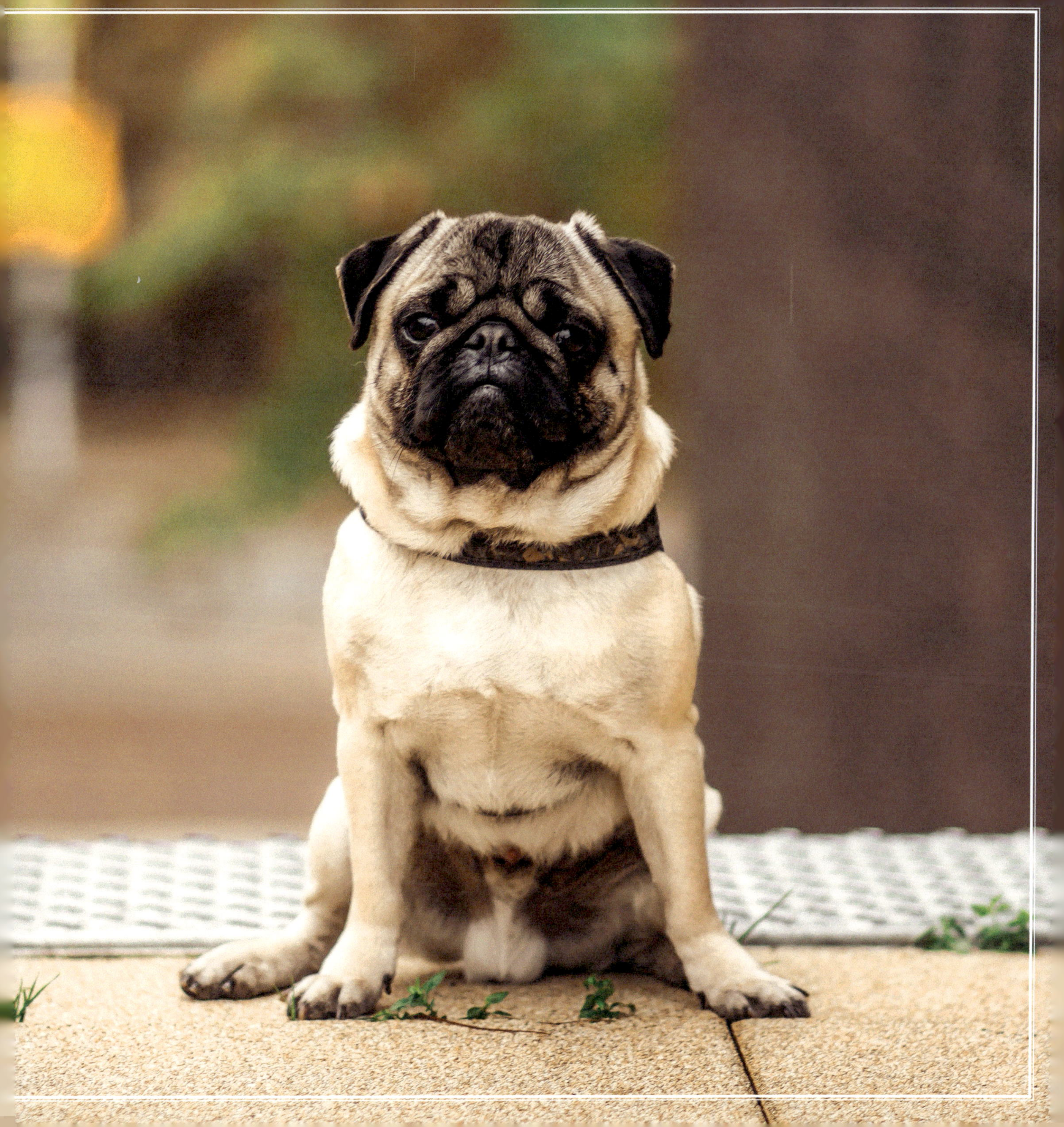

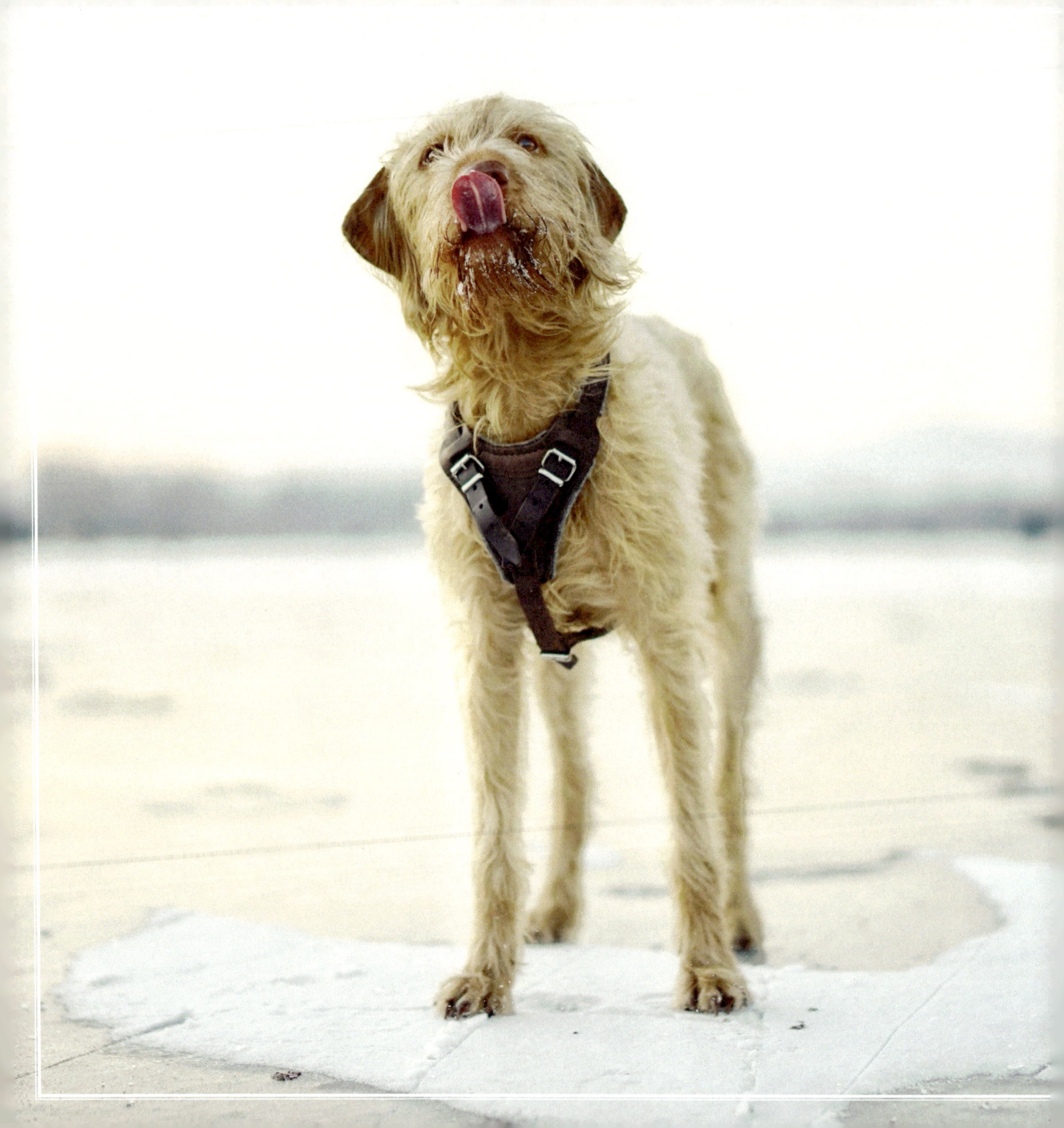

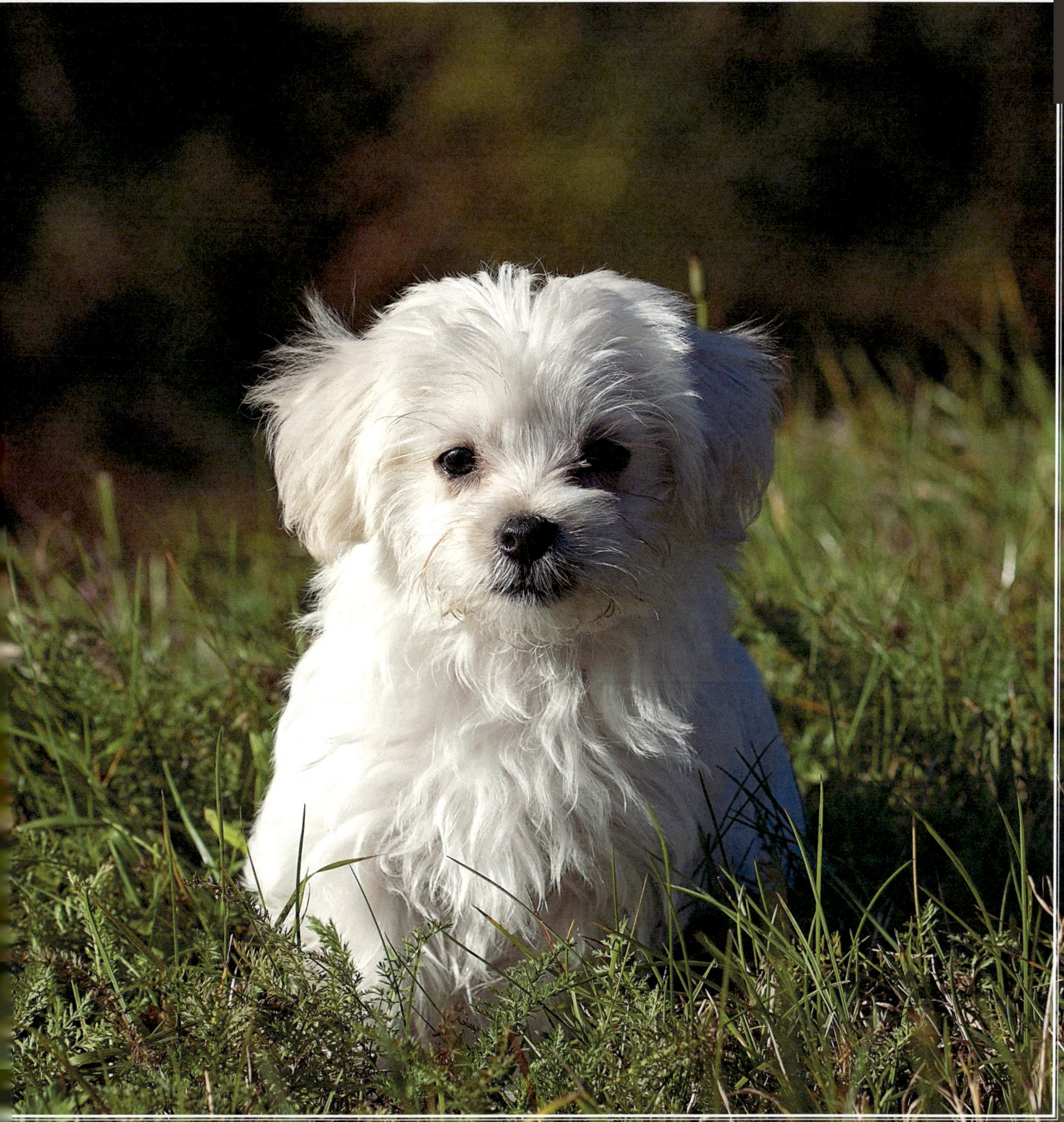

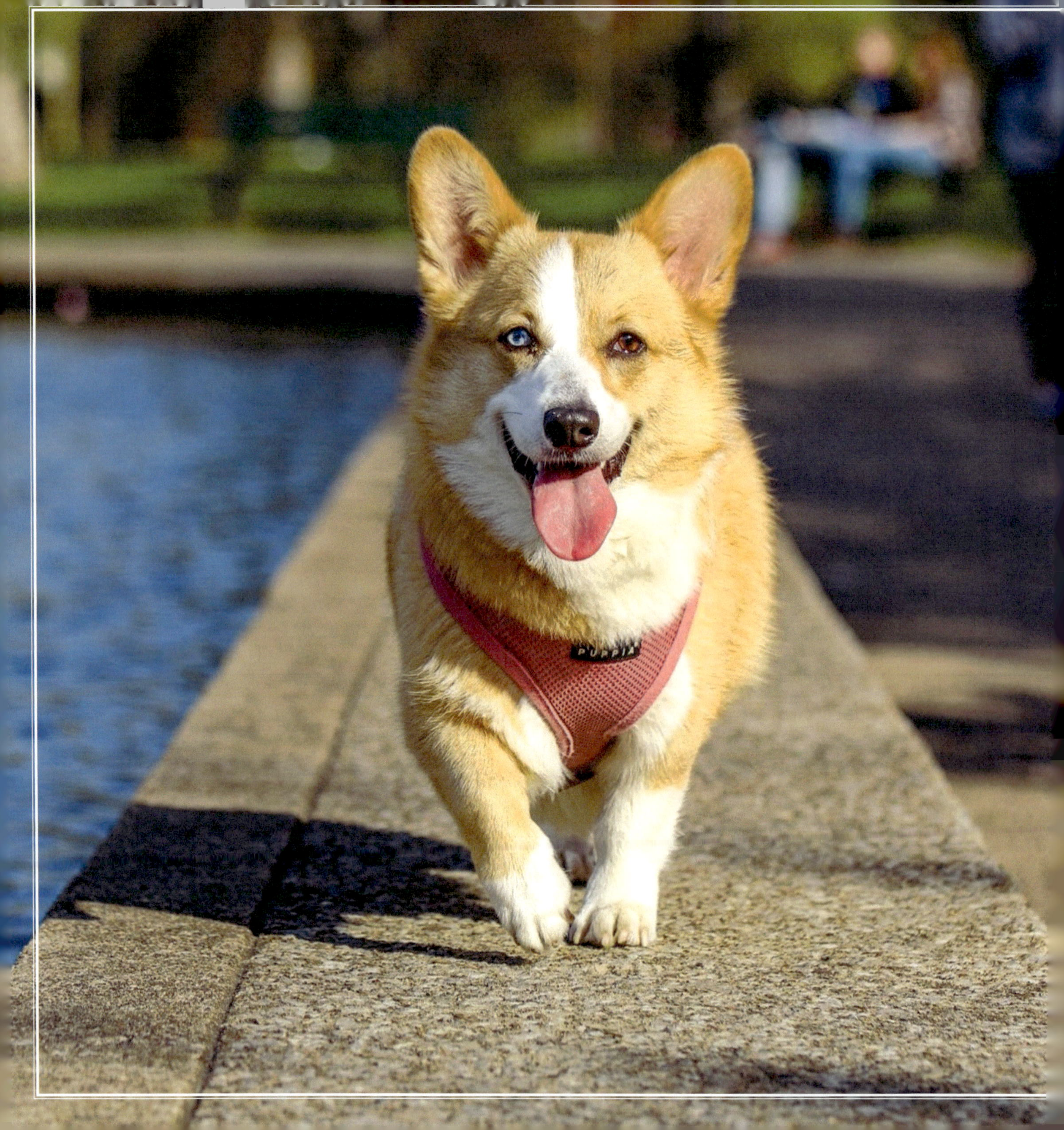
PUPPIA

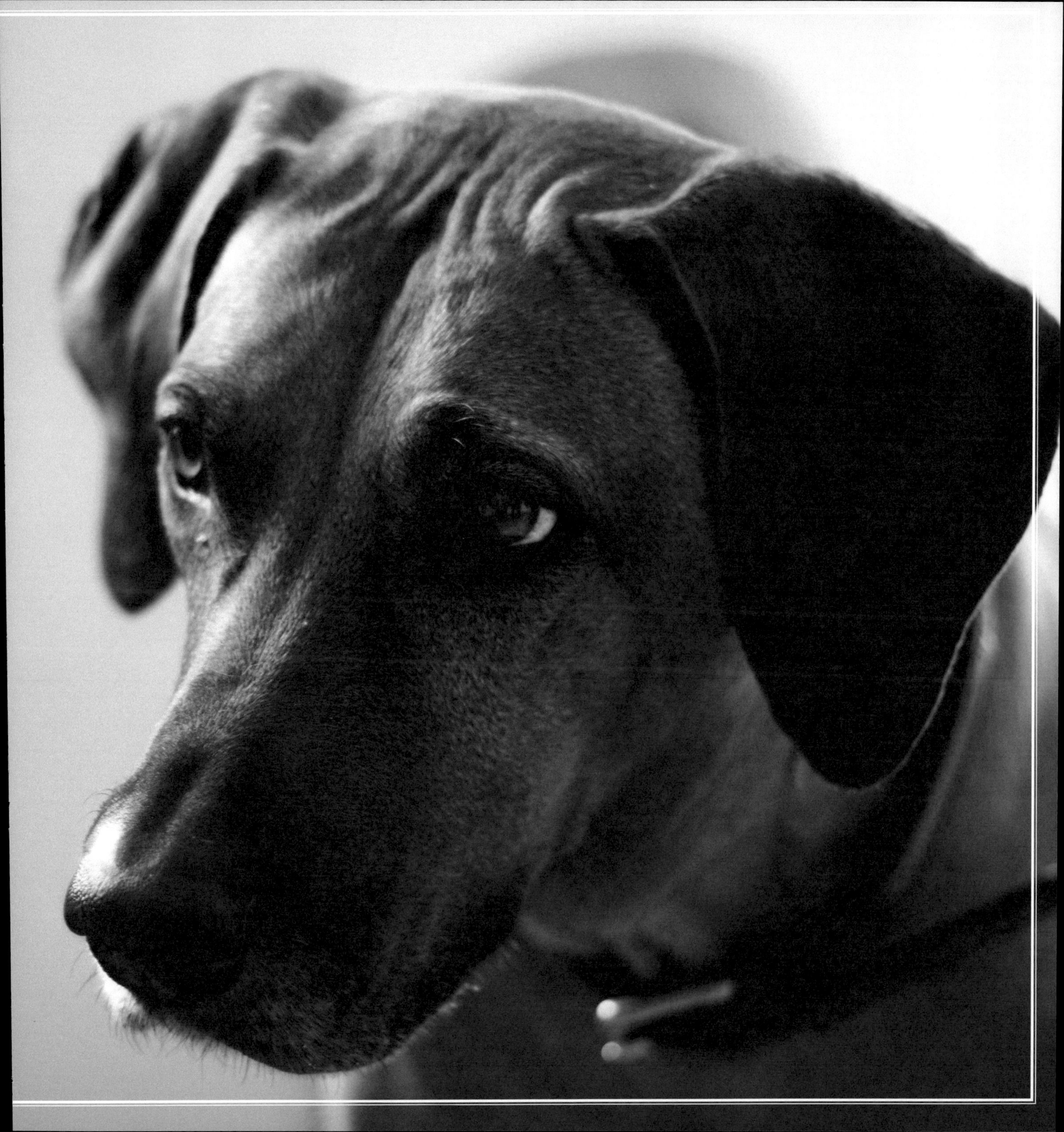

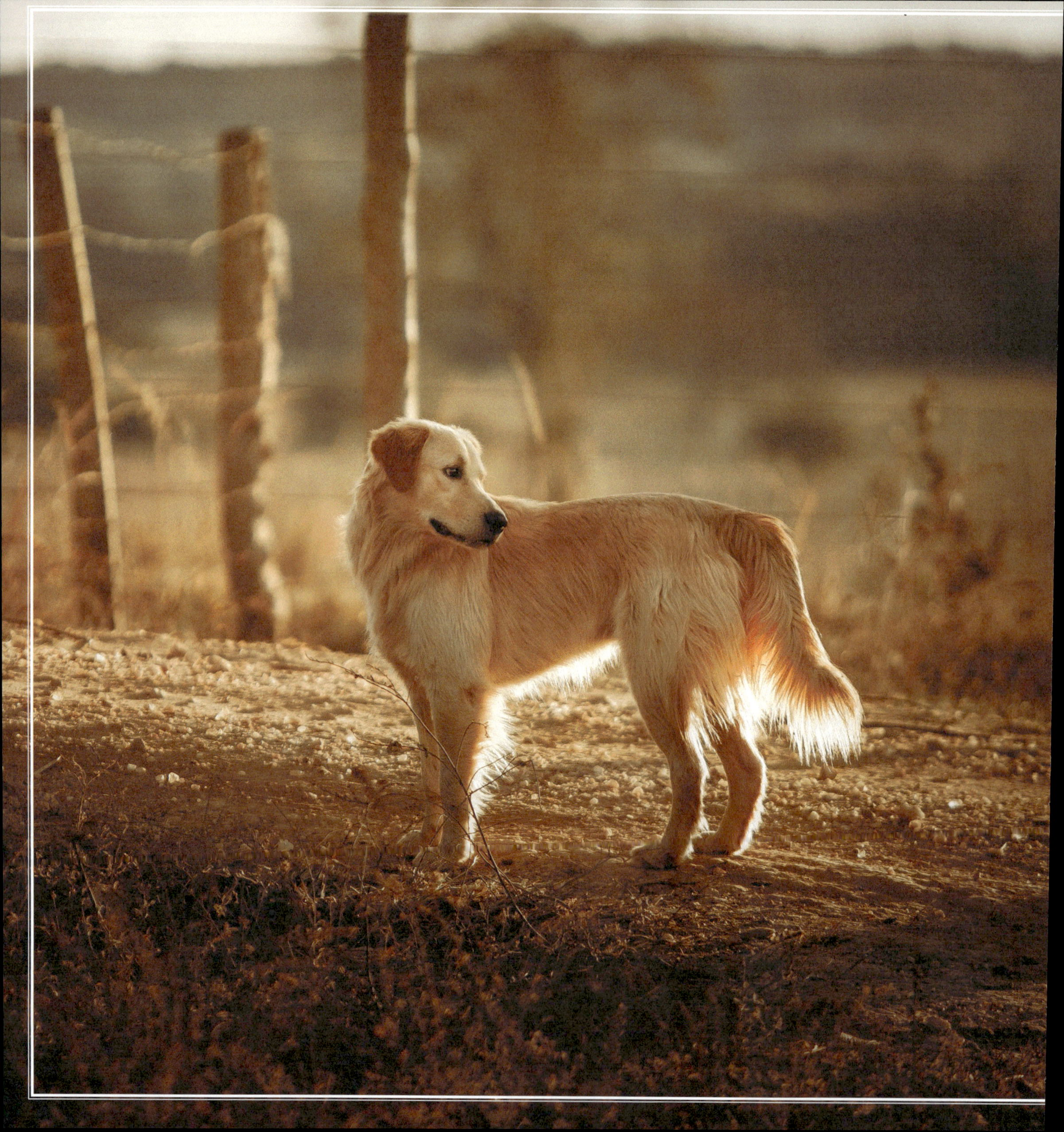

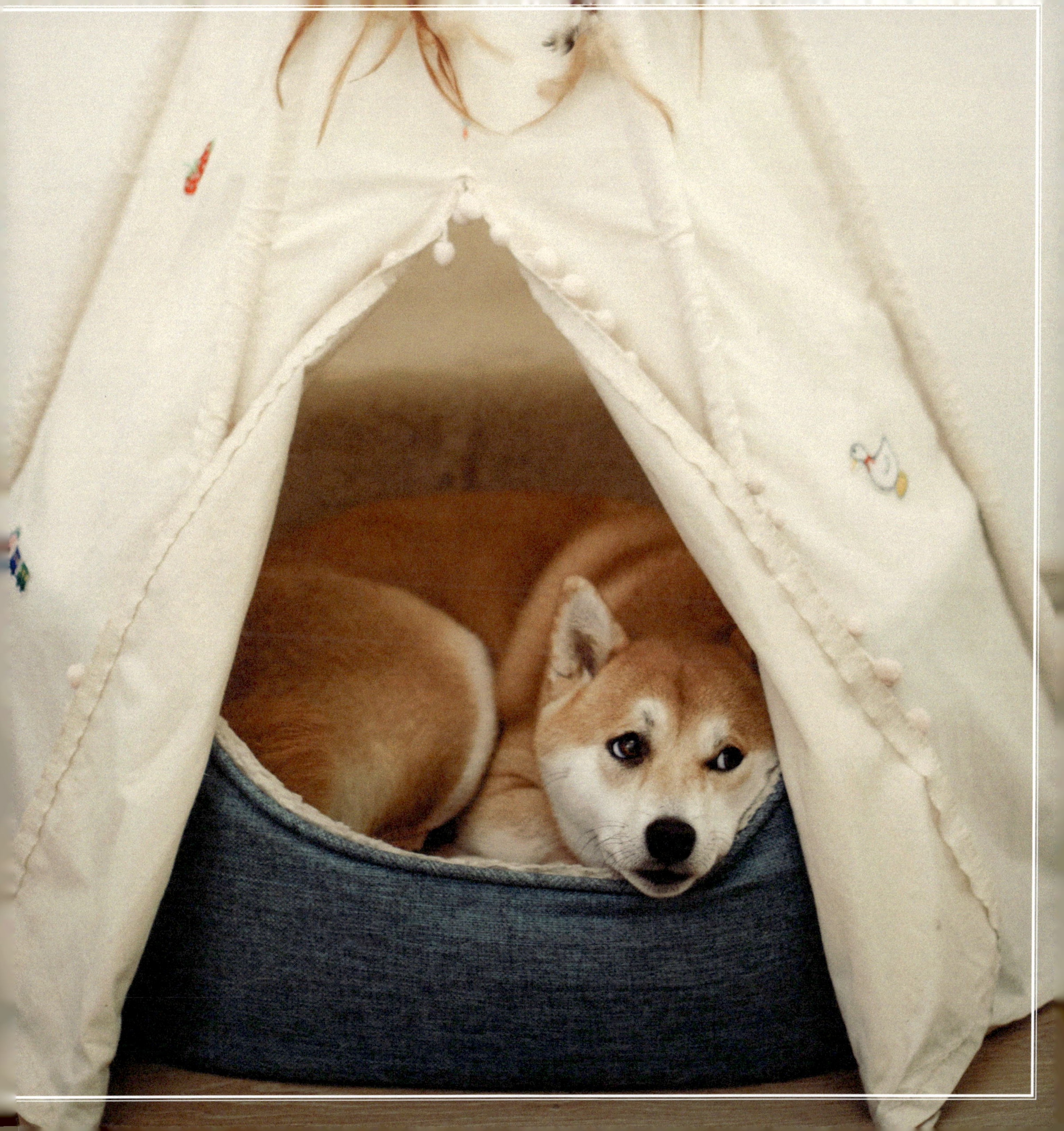

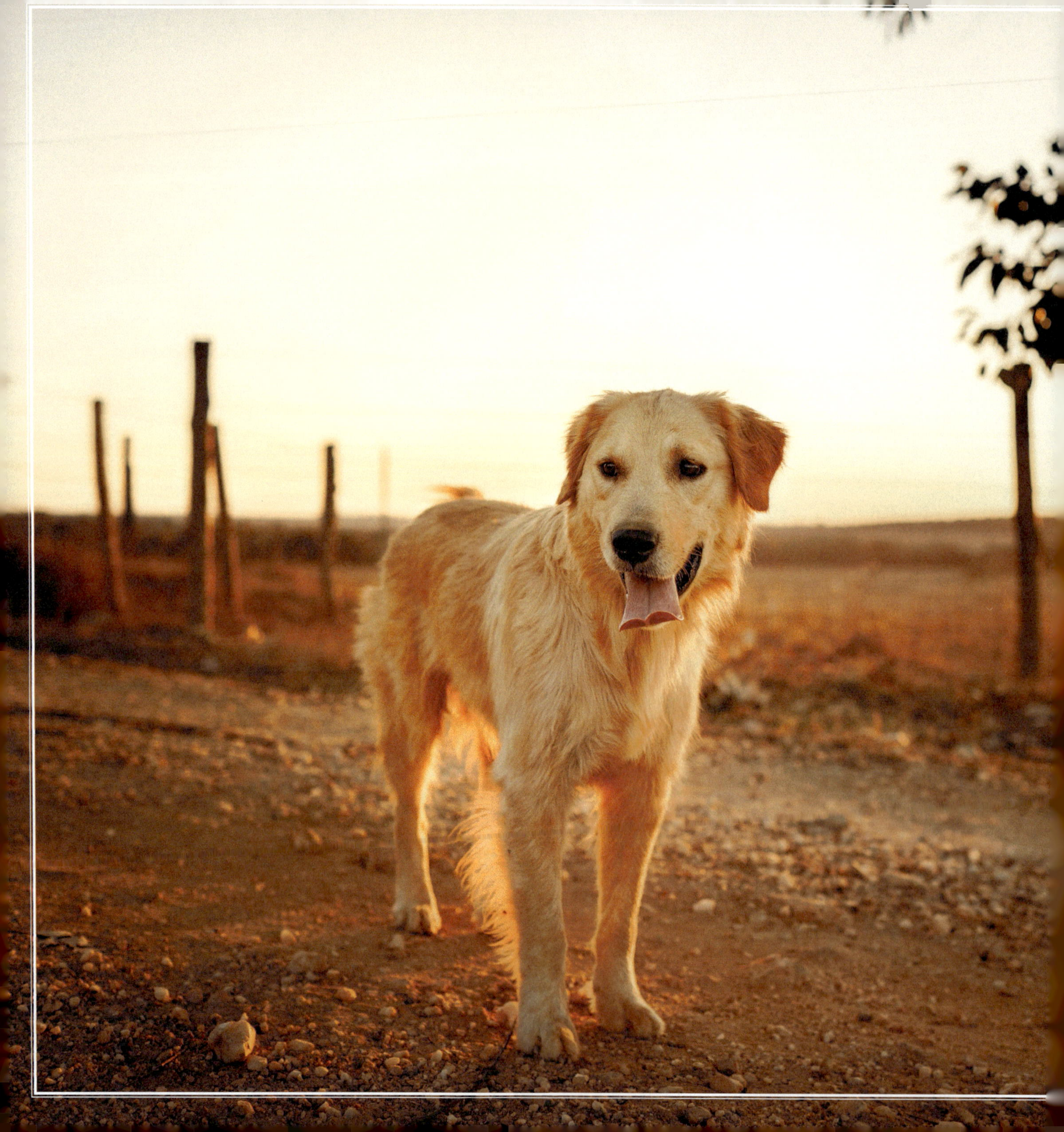

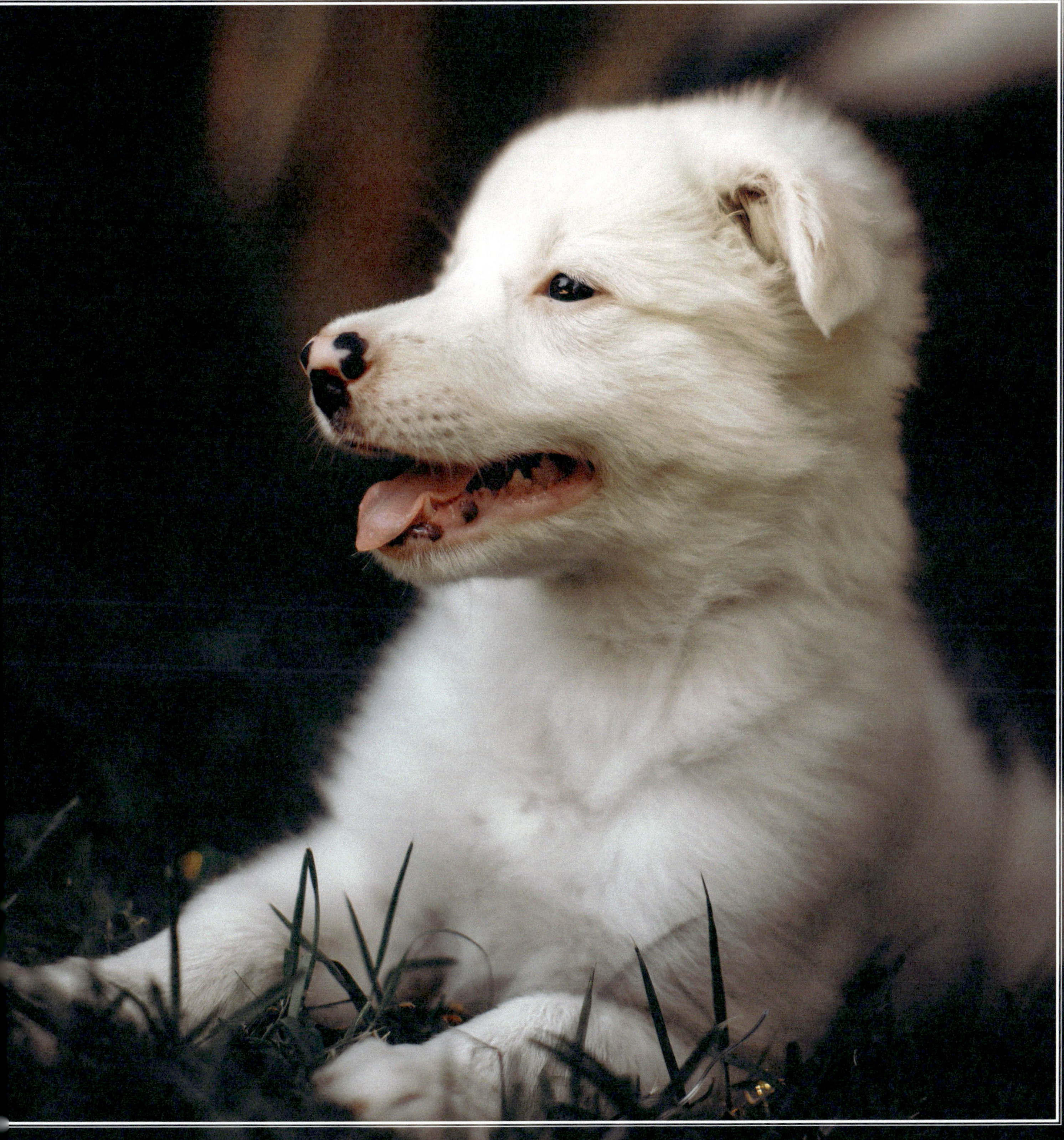

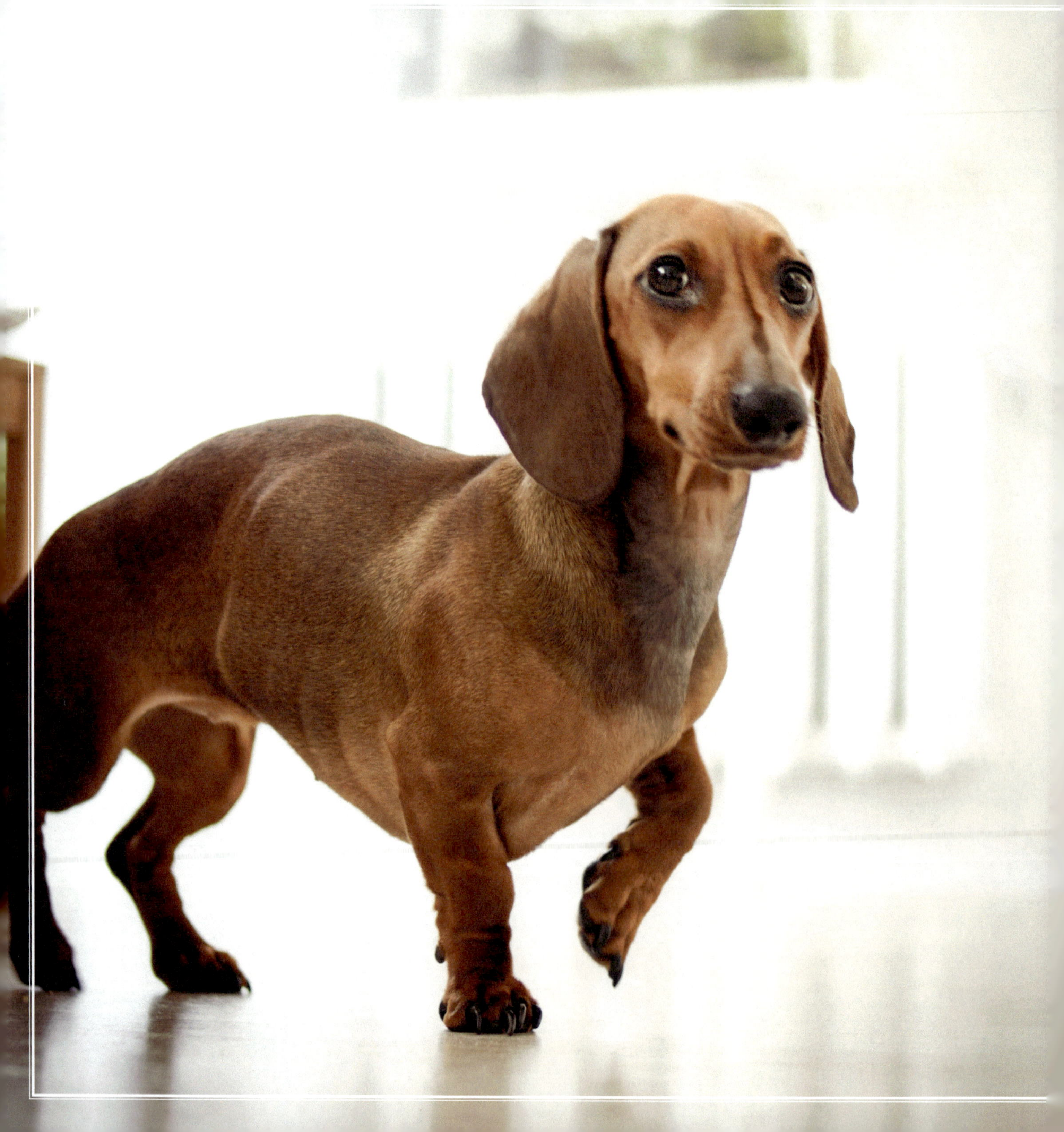

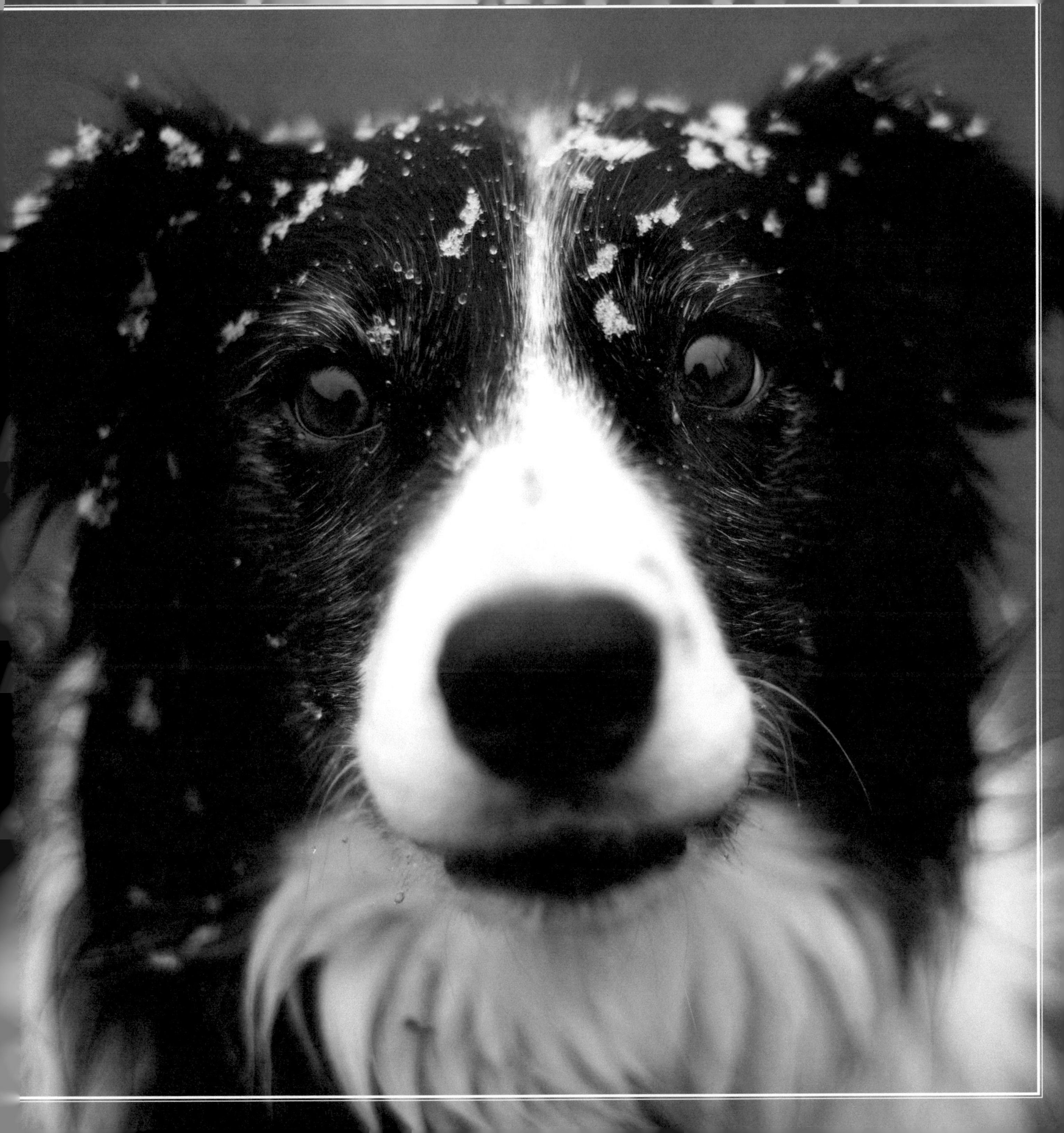

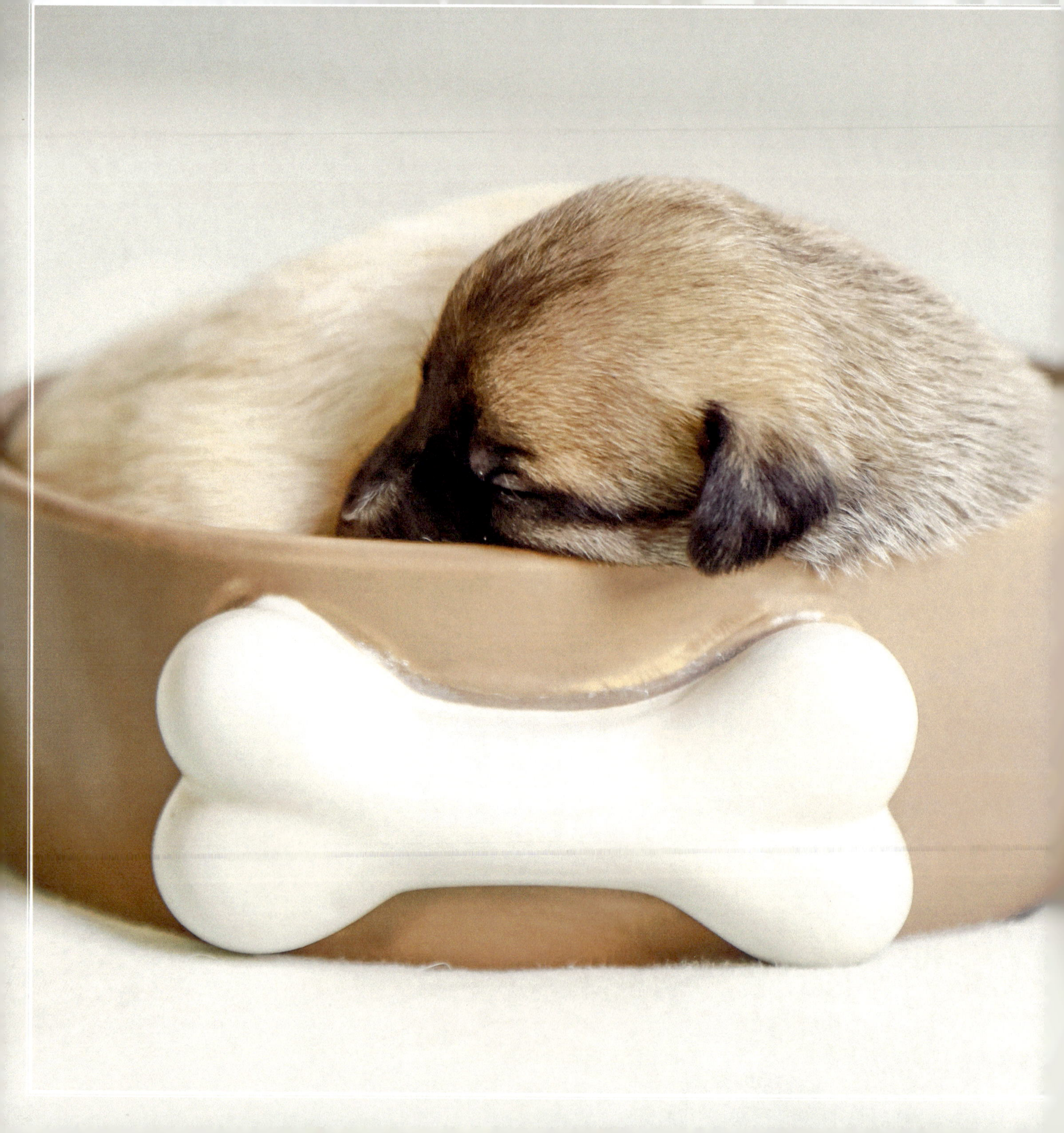

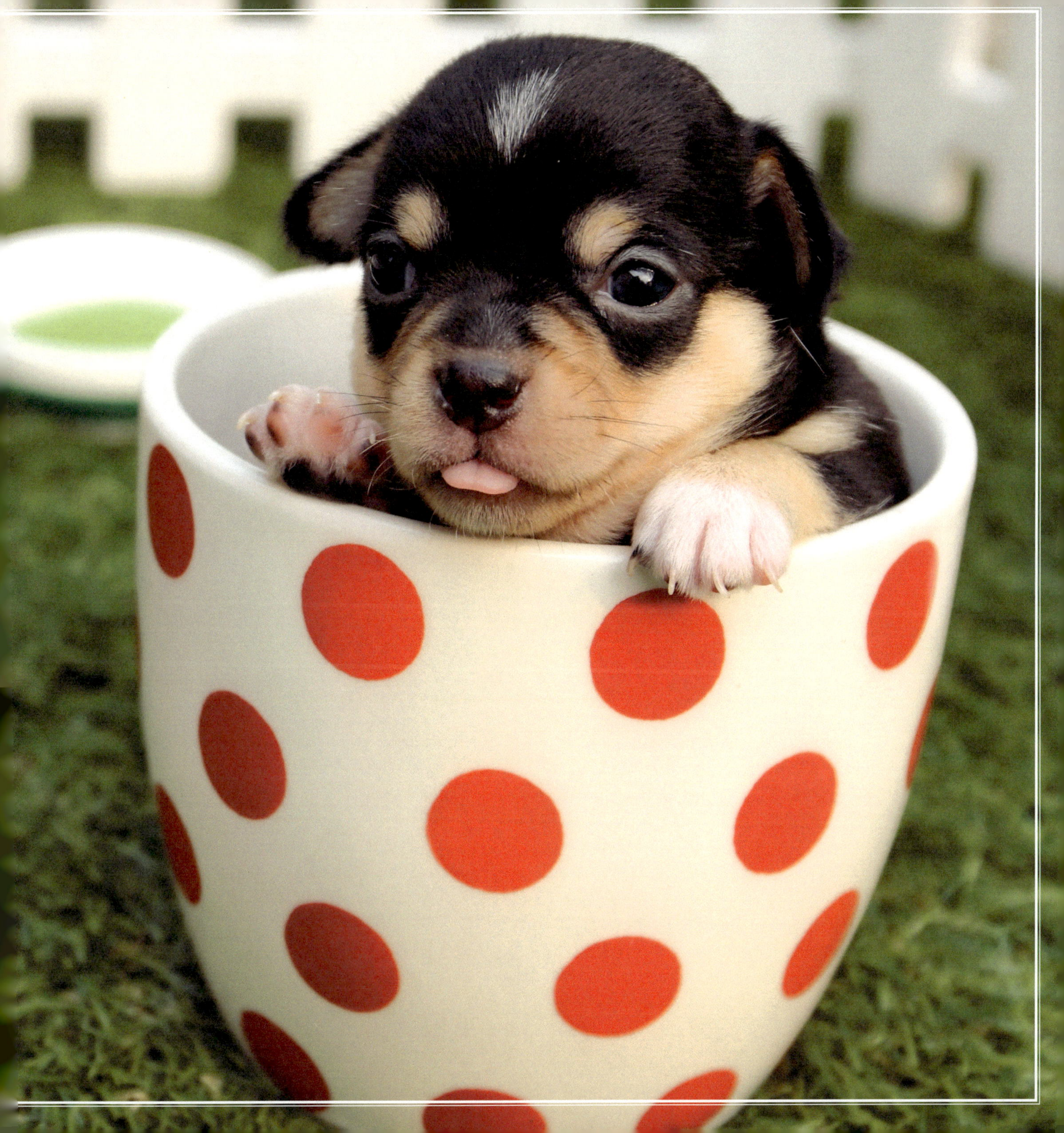

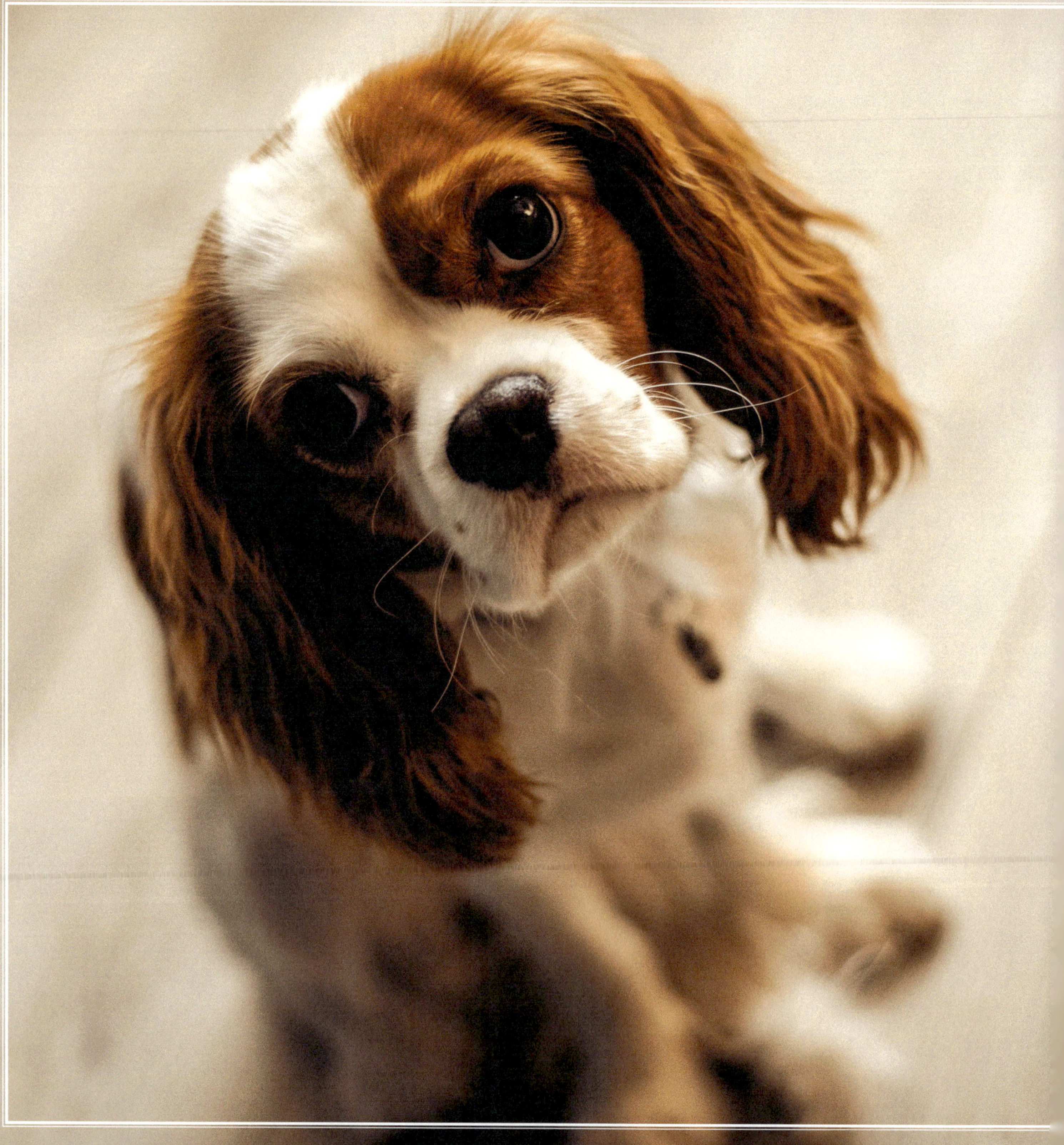

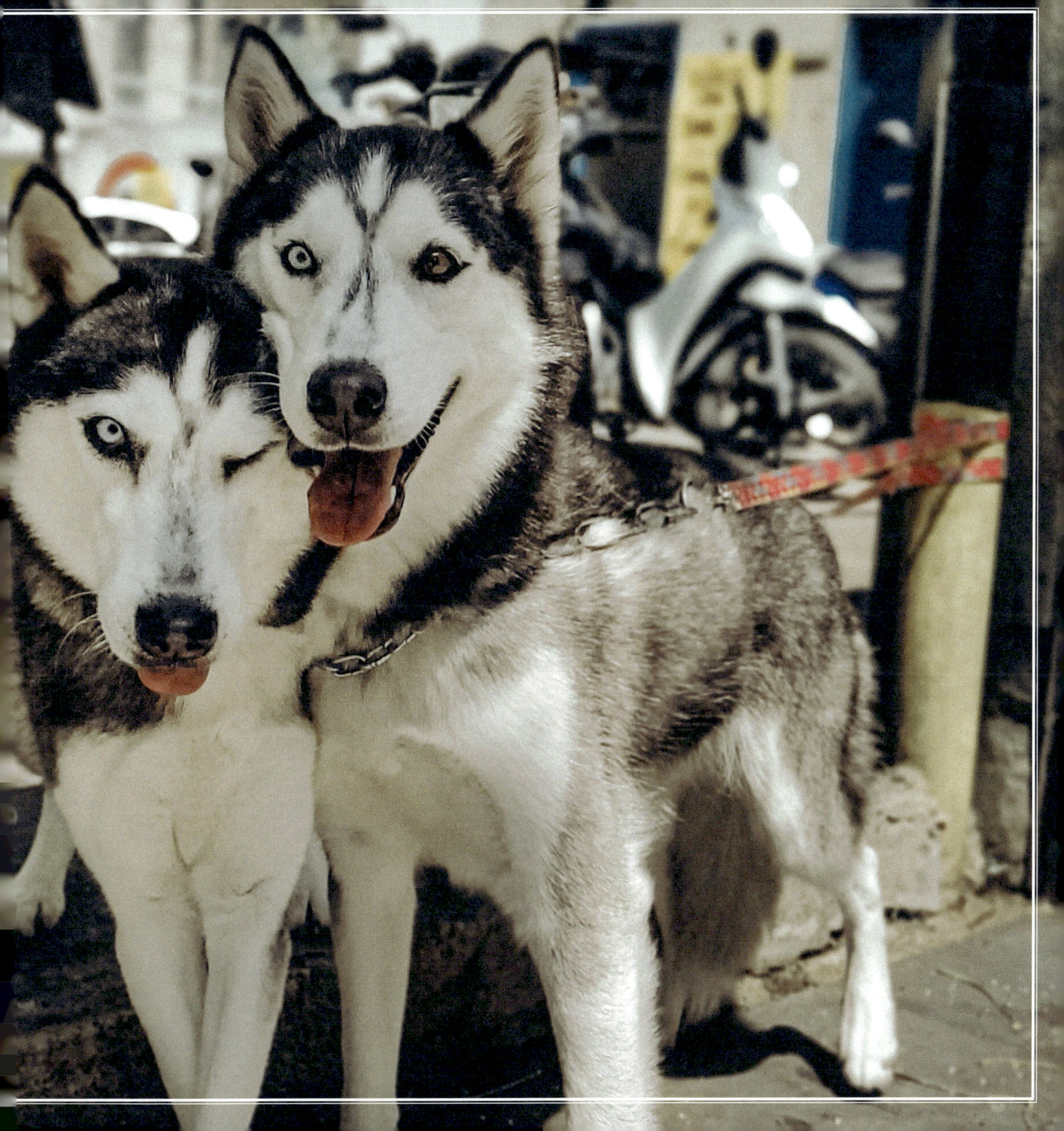

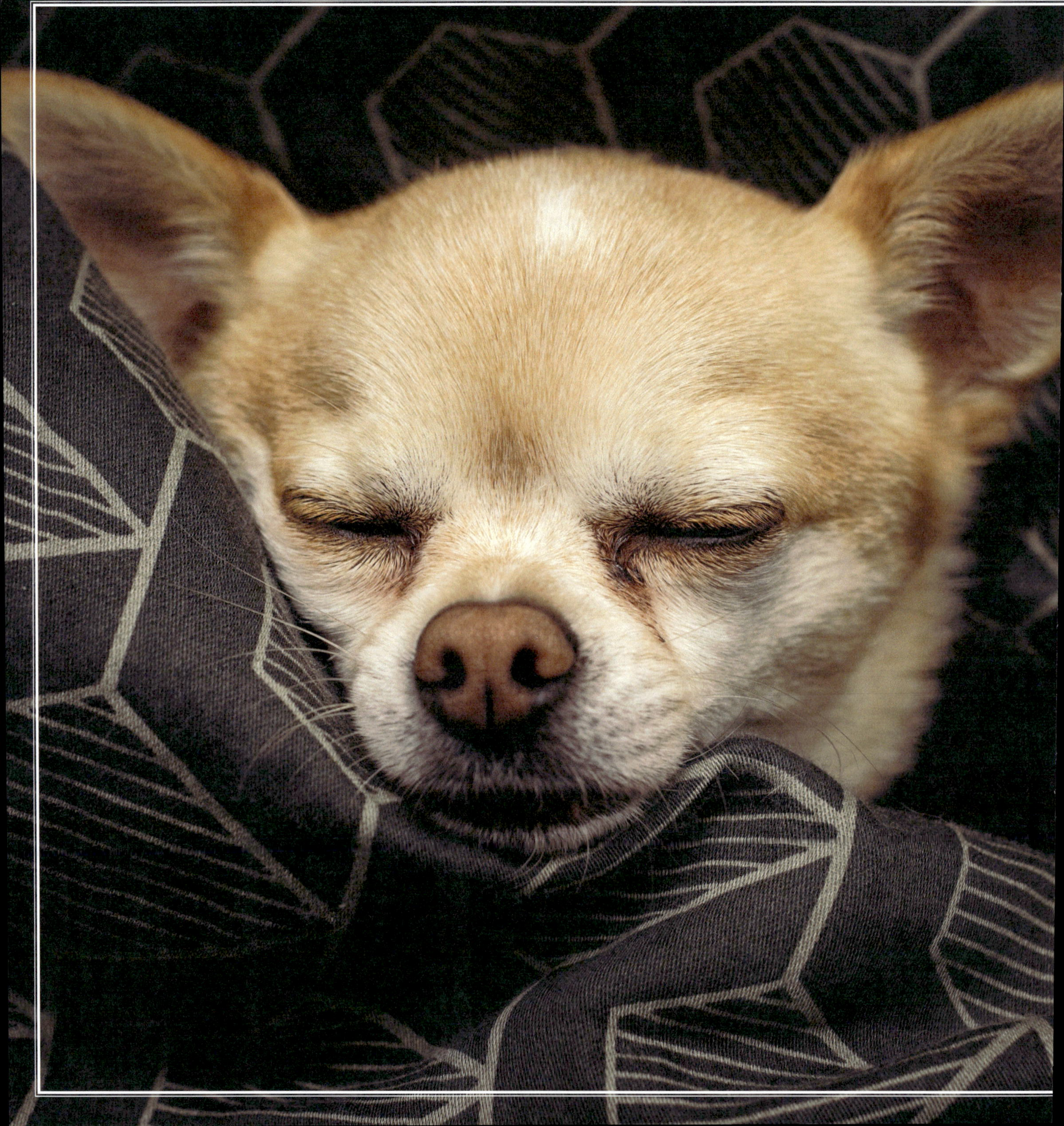

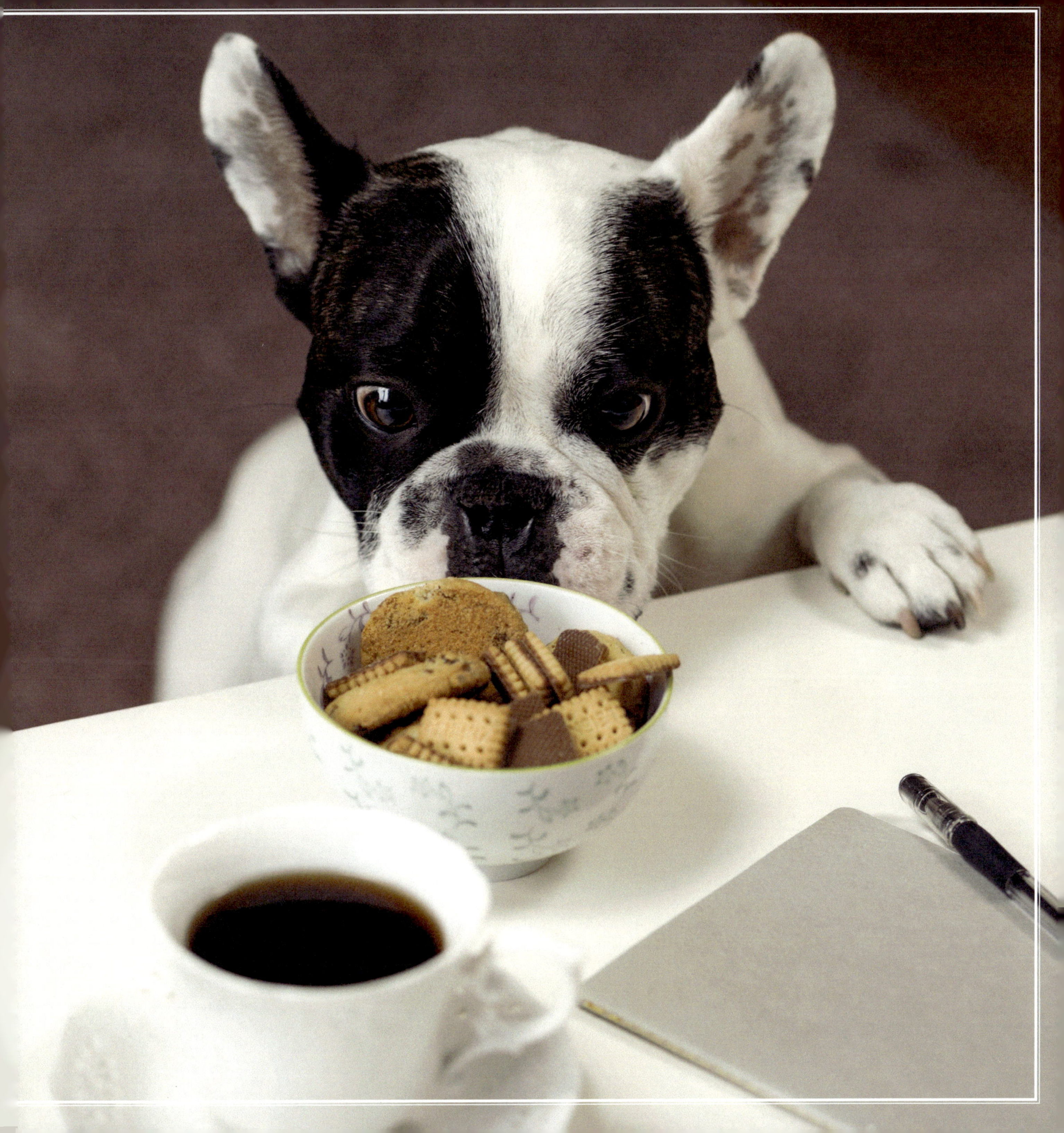

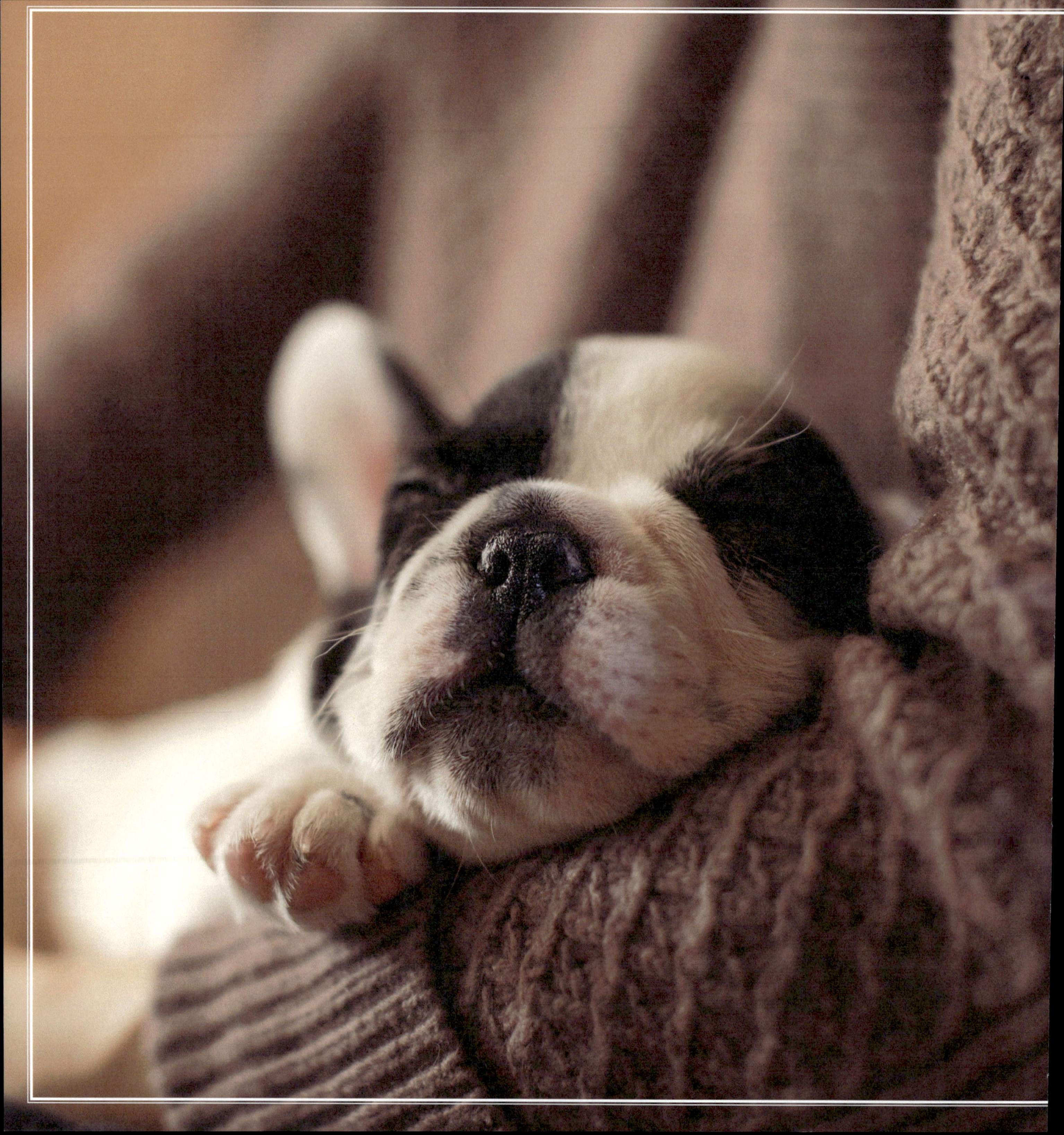

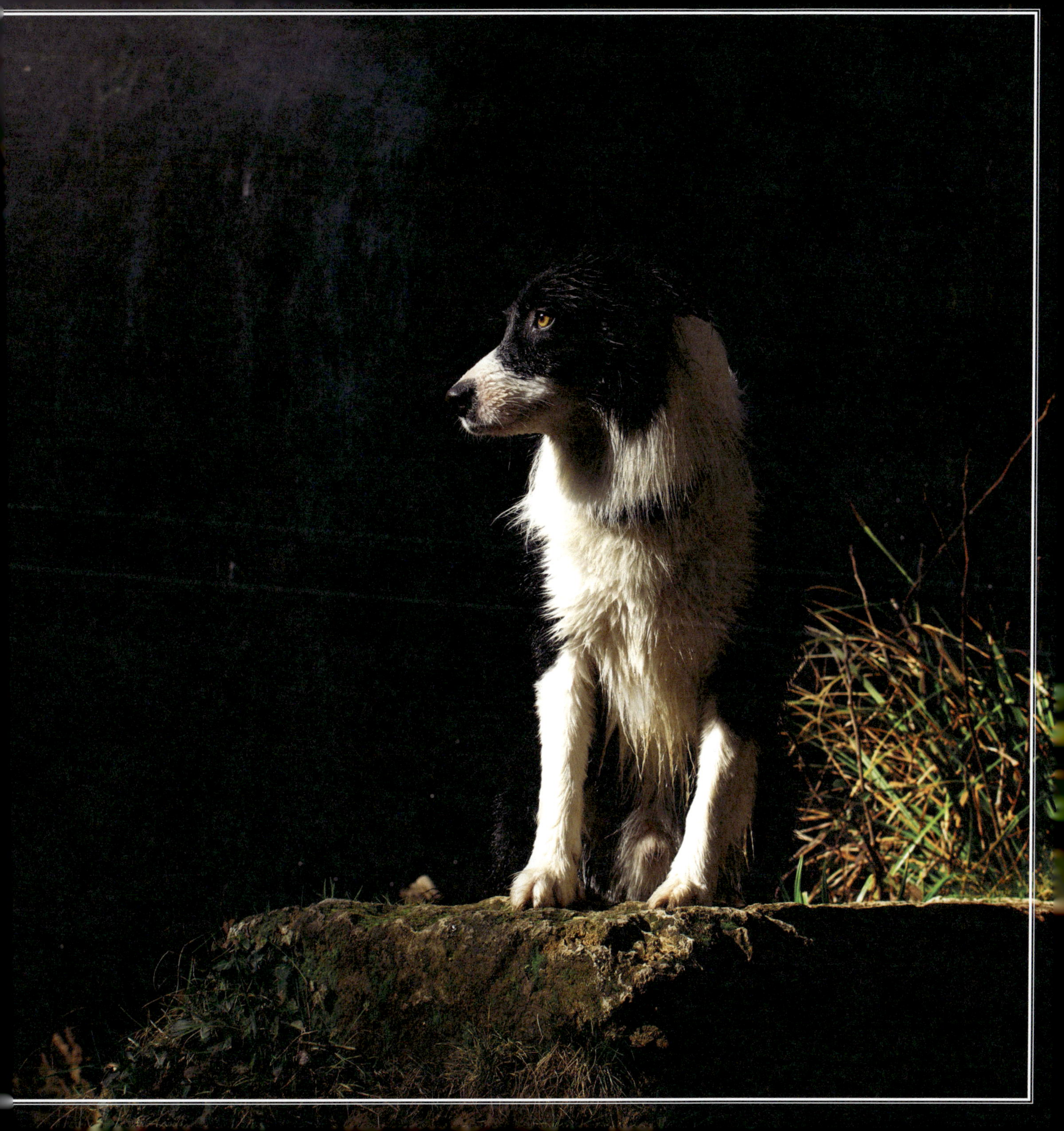

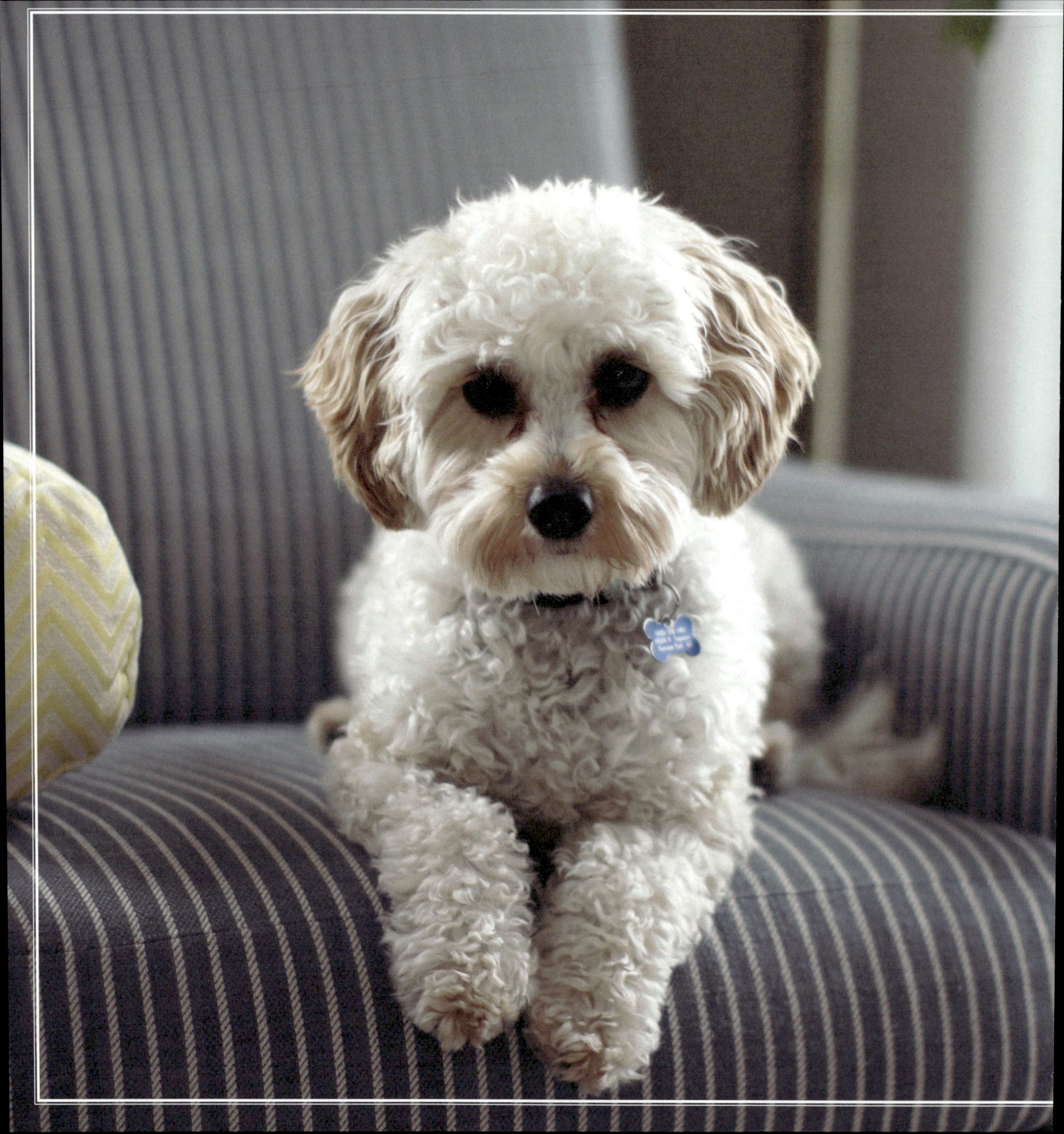

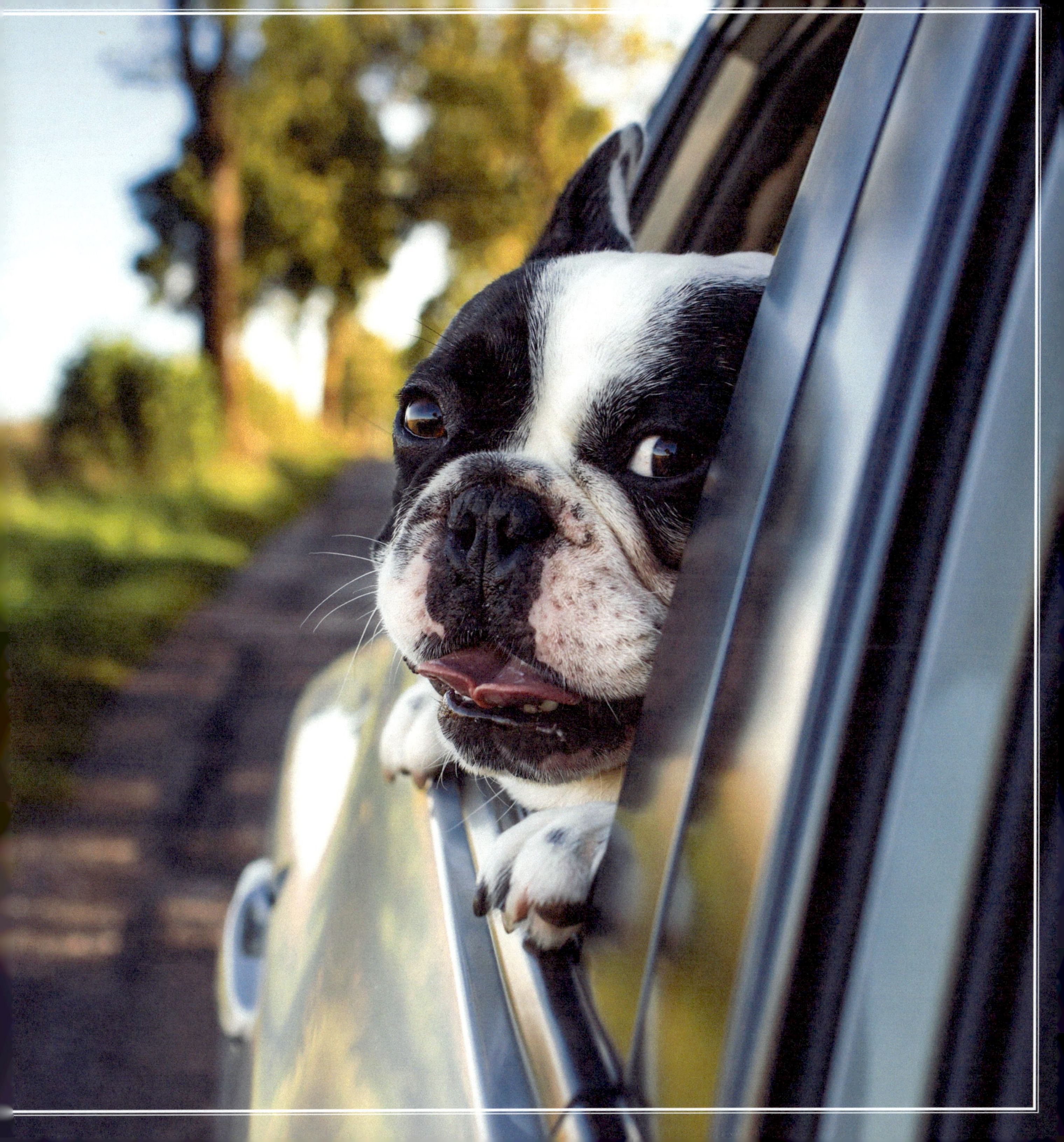

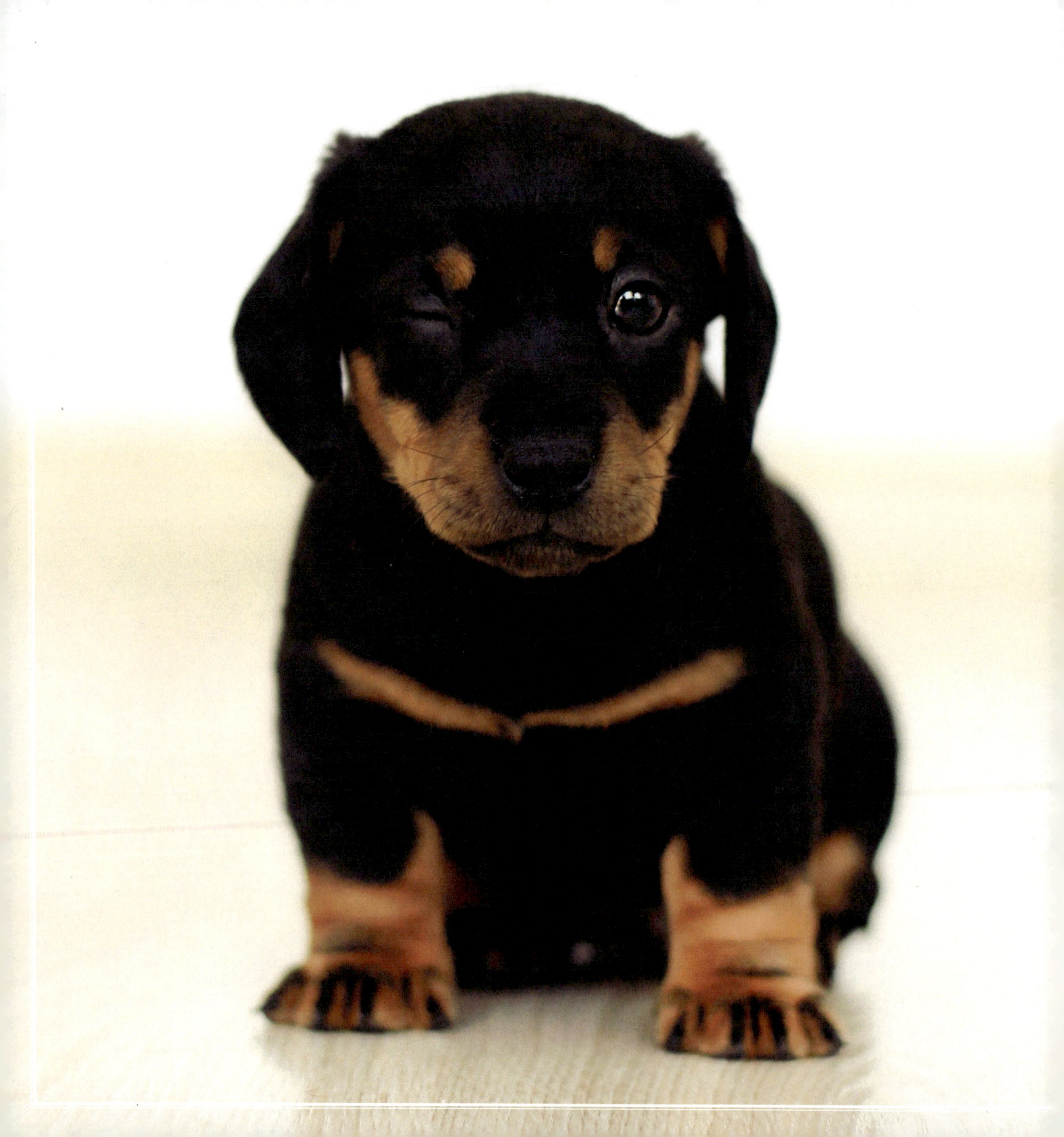

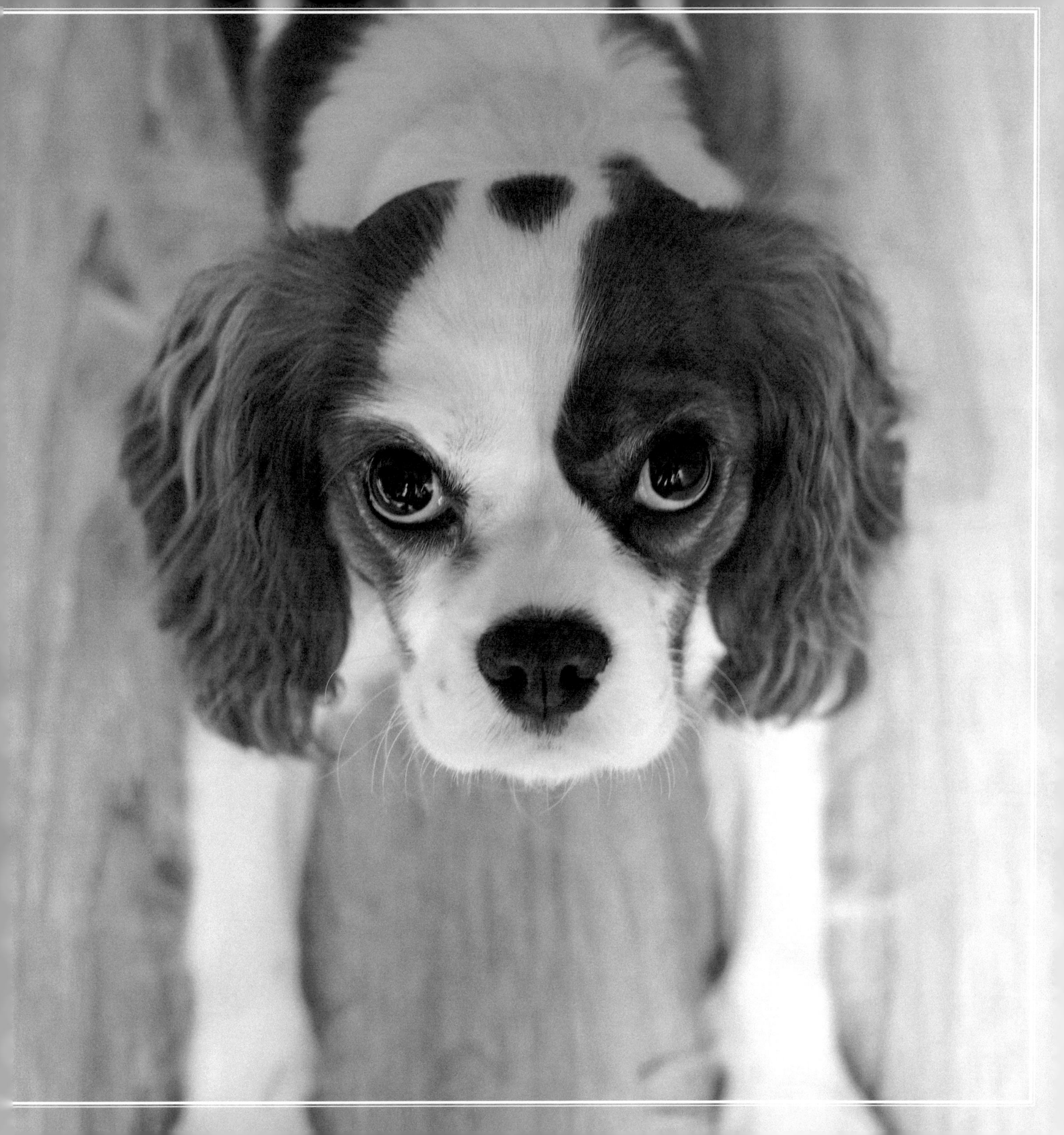

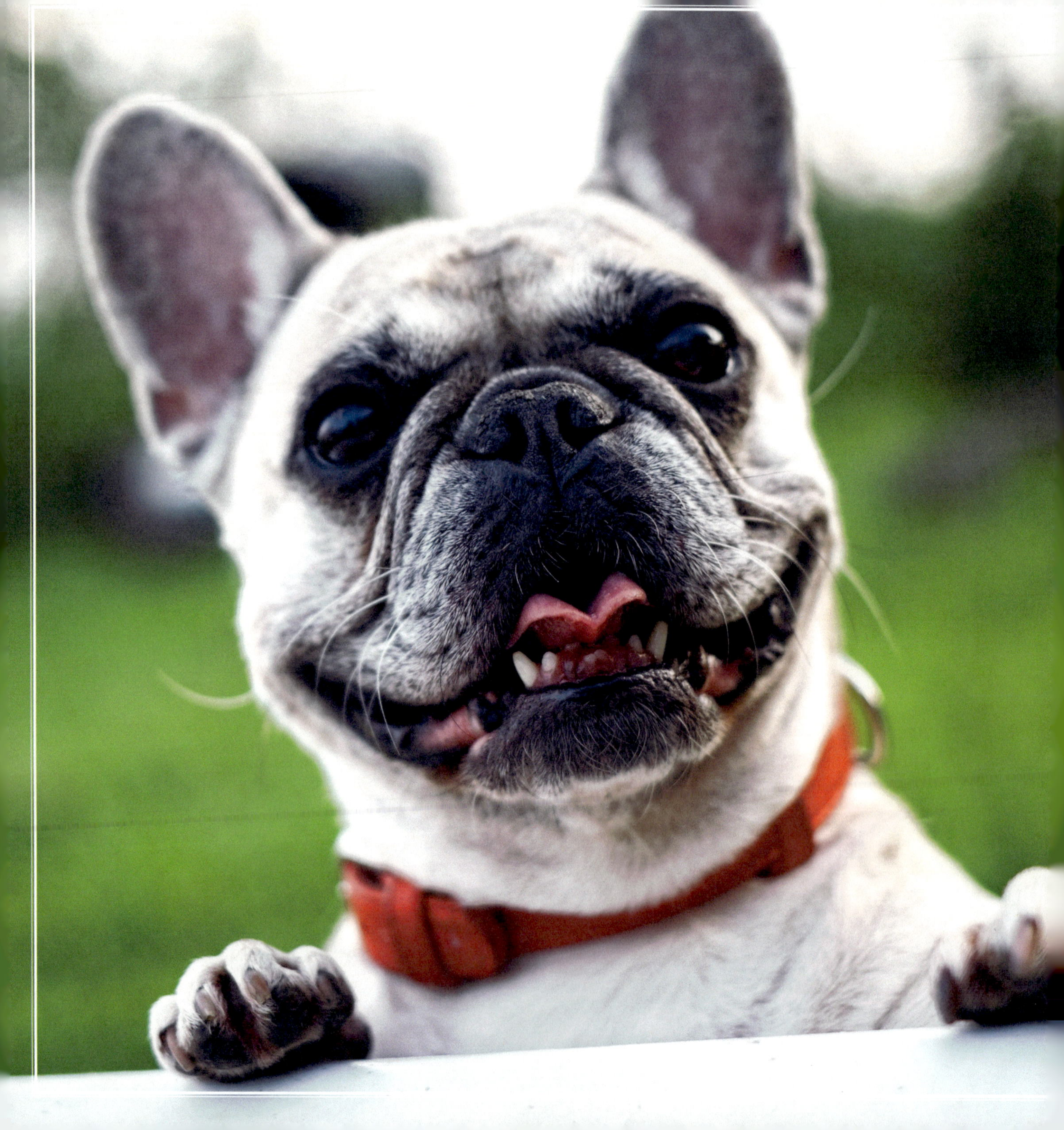

WE WOULD LOVE TO HEAR FROM YOU!

Kindly take a few minutes of your time to leave a review online at the website you purchased this book!

Made in United States
Troutdale, OR
11/24/2023

14860286R00038